D0006799

6/28

VILLANOVA UNIVERSITY
Villanova, Pennsylvania
FALVEY MEMORIAL LIBRARY

Pride and Solace

There is always a philosophy
for lack of courage.

Albert Camus,
Notebooks 1942–1951

Pride and Solace

The Functions and Limits
of Political Theory

Norman Jacobson

UNIVERSITY OF CALIFORNIA PRESS
Berkeley · Los Angeles · London

University of California Press
Berkeley and Los Angeles, California
University of California Press, Ltd.
London, England
Copyright © 1978 by
The Regents of the University of California
ISBN 0-520- 03438-4
Library of Congress Catalog Card Number: 76-52029
Printed in the United States of America

JA
81
J25

To my Mother and the Memory of my Father

449356

Contents

Prologue

IT *has been an implicit assumption within the tradition of political theory from the very beginning that the quest for truth is not identical with the quest for meaning. The writings of Plato contain hints of immutable eternal Forms, a knowledge of which may permit the philosopher to infer universal Truths. They proceed, however, by the Socratic dialectic which, in its search for meaning, supplies today's truths only to be contradicted in tomorrow's conversation. While both are present in the works of the founder of the tradition, there is no question that there has existed a preference in political theory for the true over the meaningful. The disasters of our own age only confirm the unevenness of the contest, as the "truths" established by the sciences overwhelm what humankind had so long assumed as meaningful. The concern of this book is primarily with the struggle to achieve meaning rather than to establish truth.*

The specific motif is the place of pride and solace in political theory: the pride of the theorist in the act of creation, the solace of the reader in the act of discovery. From this perspective, hardly the sole or even chief way of seeing things, the history of Western political theory is a history of various structures of solace, from the ancient Greeks to our own time. Rather than the history of solace as such, what will engage us here is an interpretation of the most persuasive structures erected in the modern age, as well as an explanation of the process by which those structures were sapped, beginning with the nineteenth century, and the way prepared for contemporary attempts at a political theory without solace.

After a general exploration of the dimension of the question before us, the structure of Machiavelli's Prince, Hobbes' Leviathan, *and Rousseau's* Social Contract *will absorb our attention. We then consider a program launched to undermine the authority of all who would construct engines of solace in the guise of political theories, and the consequences of that program. The contemporary response of George Orwell and Hannah Arendt to a political universe without meaning sets the stage for an intensive look at the Political Man of Albert Camus, unconsolable yet undaunted in spirit. A final—but by no means the last—word is addressed to the reader in a brief Epilogue.*

Perhaps a more conventional way of describing the book is to say that it examines the ascendancy in political theory of the nation-state, its subsequent decline in legitimacy, and the vulnerability of Western humanity bereft of authoritative ideas, principles, and institutions. Following the collapse of structures grown too weary to resist the fierce energies released in the Renaissance and the Reformation, men of political imagination recognized both the dangers and the possibilities inherent in the modern State and devoted to them their unstinting labor. In The Prince, *Niccolò Machiavelli was preoccupied with the acquisition of new dominions and the consolidation of political power. In his* Leviathan, *Thomas Hobbes was concerned with the achievement of order through the establishment of sovereignty. To address his subject fully, Hobbes needed to imagine a return to that period before the existence of civil society, in order to tell a somewhat different tale than Machiavelli and to play out the logic of the new State. For the origins of his State, Jean-Jacques Rousseau also deemed it necessary to reach back to a time when savage men were thought to have roamed the planet. His purpose in* The Social Contract *was to introduce into the State a heightened element of political community, the obligations and joys of citizenship. These three works, then, deal first with the acquisition of political power, then with the establishment of sovereignty, and finally with the introduction of equal citizenship.*

Hobbes and Rousseau delved deep into a mythological past to return with a specimen of "natural man" bursting with pride and a wild sort of freedom. Each would tame that creature by means of artifice, using the State he had invented. Although not imagining any human creature antedating civil society—returning to the ancient Romans was sufficient for his purposes—Machiavelli was no less intent upon taming nature. His artifice was the Prince, his challenge to learn how to act in complicity with Fortune herself in order to reduce the sway of chance in human affairs. All three, then, were engaged in fashioning an artifice to subdue nature, which is necessity.

And all three theorists were enthralled by the Biblical

*figure of the Legislator. To create the State, to breathe life
into it, and to prescribe its laws, a Legislator was indispensable. The specter of Moses haunts their pages. From
the sixteenth through the eighteenth century he is the most
persuasive model in European political theory. The great
nineteenth-century thinkers are also preoccupied with the
figure of Moses. Instead of counseling emulation, however,
they had designs upon his perpetuation as Legislator. Their
vocation as they saw it was to free us from enslavement to
all external authority. What they did was to smash the
Tables, an image after all, nothing but artifice, to release
our natural freedom suffocating under millennia of unnatural constraint, which men too fondly call culture.*

*Now it is obvious that I am describing a dream rather
than reciting political history, recounting a myth rather than
explaining anything in the "real world." But the dreamer
himself was a mythological creature, Modern Man. He
had his dream first of glory, then of peace, at last of equal
justice, a dream from which he was rudely shaken in the
fateful disenchantment of the nineteenth century. In the
theater of their imaginations, acting for Modern Man, the
greatest political theorists of the modern age deliver the
State in the sixteenth century, structure it in the seven-
teenth, bend it to human desires beyond mere necessity in
the eighteenth. Other great theorists, also acting as our surrogates, unmask the modern State and its rulers in the nineteenth, so that today we find ourselves back among the
uncertainties of the sixteenth century, vulnerable and virtually alone. Again, nothing quite like that ever did happen
—except in the consciousness of Modern Man, who sees
himself abandoned, in the eye of the hurricane, out of
which he believes he must somehow create meaning anew.*

The method employed in the book is to discover what is most at stake for each thinker, then to trace the ways by which he attempts to persuade the reader to take up his cause. The object is to think oneself inside the skin of the theorist, if he can, by paying the closest attention to the theorist's use of language and the structure he gives his work. It will be necessary sometimes even to emulate his style in order to sense the rhythms which carry us on where logic has failed the author. For what we are dealing with most often are not arguments so much as intimations, *appeals addressed to our reason but which deploy all the arts of composition to enlist our passions and prejudices in getting us to see the world from the unique perspective of the theorist.*

The great works of political theory have persisted because they are all intimations, each in its own partial way, of what persists within the political consciousness of Western humanity. No single work is complete in itself nor always objectively the same to each of us all of the time. *But together they help keep alive the richness of possibility in Western thought and experience. Plato's works might attest to our never-ending search for justice, those of Rousseau to our desire for citizenship, those of Machiavelli to our need for order. We understand these as far more than abstract ideals, however, when we turn to the greatest theorists in our different moods and circumstances. Perhaps the time to read Hobbes to maximum effect, for instance, is when we ourselves are in a fearful state. We should see soon enough just how much personal liberty we would be tempted to sacrifice in return for a guarantee of security. The great works have endured because they continue to represent us in our endless complexity and contra-*

*diction. A new political theory comes into the world when
its creator discovers still another way to capture a part of
the richness of existence.*

*Whatever else may be said of the tradition of political
theory, its contributors have sought, usually in a threatening or chaotic time, to maintain or resurrect civilized
discourse upon politics. This conversation might not have
served to discourage the determined brute from playing the
brute in politics, any more than it does today. But at the
very least, its participants have sought to keep alive standards of political judgment, always in danger of being lost
from the sight of those too preoccupied with practice to take
pause for serious thought about their own activities. It may
be true that knowledge increaseth sorrow, as Solomon believed, but it also confounds simplemindedness thrust into
action. The more we know about ourselves and other human beings, the less are we disposed to act recklessly in the
service of any set of abstract and symmetrical political principles. There are certain privileges—self-righteousness for
one—that we forsake thereby, and knowing this full well,
we are apt to fall into occasional melancholy. Perhaps that
is where the sorrow shows itself. On the other hand, he
who possesses knowledge of himself knows that he does not
know everything. And he who does not know everything
cannot kill everything. Civilized political discourse always
reinforces the lesson that none of us knows everything.*

*It has been my good fortune to have engaged in such
civilized discourse over the years at Berkeley. The respon-
siveness of generations of students, graduate and under-
graduate, as well as of numbers of sympathetic colleagues,
has been all that a participant in the ceaseless conversation*

could possibly have desired. Among those from whom I have learned far more than the mere listing of names might imply are John Schaar, Sheldon Wolin, Hanna Pitkin, Michael Rogin, Reinhard Bendix, Francis Carney, Charles Tarlton, Beryl Crowe, and Seymour Shifrin. To any others I might inadvertently have omitted, and who are able to detect traces of themselves in the pages of the book, my heartfelt thanks.

I wish also to express my gratitude to those who most influenced the specific course of development taken by the book: Benjamin Barber, who gave to an early draft an exquisite reading; Robert Peyton, who provided a wry and perspicacious one; Marilyn Schwartz, who pressed upon me the most demanding exercises in composition; and Grant Barnes, whose editorial skills were brought to bear with effortless grace.

Finally, the most precious contributions were those of my fellow seminarians of the kitchen table—Jean, Ken, Ellie, and Matt—whose talents included the restorative one of provoking me to laughter at some of my more ludicrous attempts at lifting myself by my own metaphysical bootstraps.

Berkeley   N. J.
April 1977

Chapter 1

Political Theory as Solace

I

Patriotism, religion, the Empire, the family, the
sanctity of marriage, the Old School Tie, birth,
breeding, honour, discipline—anyone of ordinary
education could turn the whole lot of them inside
out in three minutes. But what do you achieve,
after all, by getting rid of such primal things as patriotism and religion? You have not necessarily got
rid of the need for *something to believe in*.
George Orwell, "Inside the Whale" (1940)

O NE temptation through out the history of Western
political thought has been the belief that private
desperation must somehow be susceptible of public solution; that it is the office of the political theorist to be doctor
to the soul, to join in helping to relieve the conflict raging
within by projecting it outward upon the city, there to be
resolved once and for all. The conflict was sometimes
thought to be exerted by the dualism of human *nature* (man
is both flesh and spirit, body and soul), sometimes by the
dualism of human *destiny* (man is fated for his brief hour
upon the stage of the times by the dualism inherent in the
human *condition* (both creature and creator, man experi-

ences friction between what he is and what he makes). However an age or a people actually perceived the contradiction, it has spurred political theory to a whole series of spectacular attempts at resolution in the public realm. Only, resolution has had a way of resembling more a triumph of one term to the contradiction, or more properly, the sacrifice of one to the other.

Machiavelli knew men to be mostly treacherous, mostly selfish and deceitful; to be sure, they were also quite capable of generosity and even of friendship. But a unified Italy would be possible only by a superior deployment of treachery, selfishness, and deceit. According to Hobbes, man exhibits many traits, ranging from pride to fear; but let us not count too heavily upon any save fear. It was fear which contained the dynamism sufficient to rouse men out of their perilous and mutually destructive bestiality, and it was fear alone which would permit the commonwealth to flourish in peaceful industry. To "put oneself first is an inclination natural to man," Rousseau said; but he also said that the "sentiment of justice" is an "inborn" trait. To be saved, we must learn to discipline our selfishness and place it at the disposal of the sentiment of compassionate justice, now expressed in the General Will. Resolution is once more purchased for us, and at the customary price.

The political theorist has been tempted, then, deliberately to blind himself to certain of the "facts of life." But when he has actually yielded, the impulse has appeared less deception than desperation. When the tension has mounted unbearably and man becomes a danger to himself and his fellows, who then will maintain the human community, or recreate it? Political theory has been a heroic business, snatching us from the abyss a vocation worthy of giants.

Once Plato gave to the world his blueprint for an ideal state, the goldrush was on. Plato's was not only the first and most compelling blueprint, but became the model for most subsequent attempts at resolution. As a model it sought to solace man, to put him at peace with himself, to ease the destructive effects of the dualism raging within by prescribing a life in accordance with the dictates of reason. In *The Republic* Plato has Socrates tell Glaucon that "poetry feeds and waters the passions instead of drying them up; she lets them rule, although they ought to be controlled, if mankind are ever to increase in happiness and virtue." The key word is *controlled*. It is for control of the passions which threaten to irrupt into public life that society exists. The state itself thus resembles a vast dehydrating plant for "drying up" the passions of men through education and constraint. The figure employed by Plato is a constantly shifting one: if sometimes the words of the theorist are placed at the service of botanical metaphors or crude hydraulic ones, on other occasions they may become therapeutic in character. Nor is Plato willing to relinquish even the powers of magic to achieve his end—which is, ironically, the triumph of austere rationality. Socrates's very argument "shall be a charm to us, which we will repeat to ourselves while we listen to her [poetry's] strains; that we might not fall away into the childish love of her which captivates the many." Plato has Socrates devise a spell, an incantation distilled from the pure essence of poetry itself, namely, his own rhetoric, to protect the potential victim against poetry's fatal charm. Socrates's argument serves as an amulet to all the subjects in the Kingdom of Reason, a lorica to ward off the Devil, the stuff with which to block up their ears against the terrible seductiveness of the Siren song. Only Socrates, or Plato himself, enjoys the ecstasy—and experiences the terror—of that song. The first systematic political theory in the West is, then, not only a heroic but also a prideful business.

Not poetry, not the expression of the passions, but philosophy is to be the Ruler. The "arts of measuring and numbering and weighing," Socrates says, "come to the rescue of the human understanding—there is the beauty of them," and appearance is forced to "give way before calculation and measure and weight." The point is not that philosophy must *also* have a voice in the conversation, but that "the rational principle of the soul," as Socrates called it, must control the terrifying powers at work in the human heart. Perhaps no commentaries on Western humanity are so telling as its first great political theories. The inventions of the Greeks Pascal regarded as rules laid down for the governance of "a lunatic asylum." Or if you prefer Max Beerbohm: "So this is Utopia? Well, I thought it was hell."

From Plato's time, our theorists have been preoccupied with schemes designed to defend us against either the wantonness of our passions or the frailty of our reason. And each system seems to have involved something of a sacrifice. That there has been no enduring agreement in the critical matter of what is to be saved and what cast away should come as no surprise. As we know only too well, one man's utopia is very likely to prove another man's hell. Still, the quest went on. And the rhythm—perhaps I should even say the ritual—of classic works remained unchanged, however varied the content or style and however disparate the political circumstances. First, the author heightens the terror in the hearts of his readers by exposing in a wholly new way their fears as stemming, not from anything within themselves, but from the particular political condition. That is, he names men's dread. Then he offers them his gift of public resolution.

Only today, we witness a startling rupture in the classic pattern. The political or social scientist offers his solutions, but without having first engaged us: he is Plato unaffected by the death of Socrates. When the artist is a master at evoking an aura of sheer terror, but has no apparent civic interest in striving for our release, or no capacity for it, we have Aeschylus's *Orestes* without the intervention of Athena.

For modern man, our oracles tell us, the term "human nature" has no objective content. All we are entitled to talk about is the "human condition." In the good old days there had existed fixed principles grounded in authoritative definition. Older, philosophic anthropologies had presented definitions of man with built-in limits. We knew at once what was distinctively human. But our newer, naturalistic anthropologies merely tell us that man is the tool-making animal, the symbol maker, the great-brained one. And that is all. They set no limits to political action, and offer no reasons for limits other than the more or less pragmatic ones which fail to carry us very far. The peculiarly "modern" analytic perspective, then, is the view of man and of politics in which they are seen to exist in the absence of definite limits. In fact, some writers would settle upon this sort of statement as almost a definition of "modernity."

Hence totalitarianism, hence colonialism, hence nationalism, Stalinism, Nazism, fascism, racism. The unique preoccupation of the sensitive modern is with the possibility of establishing limits to action in the face of the dilemma, the possibility of making something out of nothing, of having the person himself import meaning into his own existence as a private human being and into his activities as a member of the political community.

While I share the concern, I cannot agree exactly with the diagnosis. I must reject specifically the romantic idea of the sound comfortable wholeness of the past, the notion that older political theories have always built upon settled views of the "nature" of man in distinction to the excruciating modern business of trying to create something out of the void of the human "condition." I simply cannot bring myself to credit the idea that any political theorist worthy of the name came fully equipped with an unalterable foundation upon which to erect a system of limits. *For all great theorists there has always been a sense in which the civic god is dead.*

The familiar world of Plato was everywhere threatened by collapse. The old values had succumbed, character was uncertain, public life increasingly tenuous. The myth was dying, Socrates was dead. Plato must write, must resurrect the old myth in the guise of a new discipline, for the salvation of the city.

Has the political theorist always been cast in the role of Grand Inquisitor rather than Prophet, of comforter rather than questioner? I am persuaded that whatever his sorrow he has accepted the role graciously, and with some modest hope. After all, there can be only one Jesus, one Socrates.

But the authors of the Gospels, and Plato, and . . . Moses? Now there was a figure to be emulated, the most celebrated of all Legislators, a man whose laws outlived not only his own lifetime, but even that of the formal nation they had brought into being. Machiavelli, Hobbes, Rousseau—practically all political theorists until the nineteenth century were of the company of Moses. Only later was the Legislator studied in order to be disarmed.

Machiavelli, Hobbes, Rousseau: each had been convinced of the existence of unprecedented corruption or the immanence of destruction, and enthralled by the possibilities of Legislation. Take Thomas Hobbes. Hobbes was born at the approach of the Armada, survived a period of violent civil war, plague, and the devastation of the Fire of London. He witnessed "fixed principles" endlessly displaced: Anglican, Puritan, Presbyterian, Catholic. Given Hobbes' desperate longing for peace, as well as his urbane disenchantment with all religious superstition, it is reasonable to assume that he would gladly have become a Christian, any sort of Christian, were he convinced that Christian principles were sufficient first to establish, then to maintain the social peace. It was precisely because he was persuaded that neither traditional Christianity nor Humanist learning was equal to the task, that Hobbes sought to enthrone his new god, the Sovereign, and to found his new civic religion inspired by political geometry.

The notion that in the past men had been supported by unshakable principles while modern man thrashes about over his head, groping for a life raft, is a common but not always justifiable notion. Behold Classical Man: he lives in a Classical house, attends Classical tragedy, contemplates

Classical art, listens to Classical music, is absorbed in Classical politics, solaced by Classical religion—all based on fixed Classical principles. Only, Plato appeared not to have seen it exactly that way. Or take another trophy down from the shelf, the simple, happy-go-lucky serf of the Middle Ages, secure in the knowledge that justice reigns in the universe. There he is, bowing and tugging at his forelock, in a lively effort to impress his Lord and Bishop that he himself wishes nothing so much as to have them keep things that way. We hear him say, it's splendid to be a simple, happy-go-lucky Medieval Man, secure in the knowledge that justice reigns in the universe. Or, it's splendid to be a Gothic Man, a Renaissance Man, an Enlightenment Man, even a prosaic Victorian Man—provided we can for a moment forget some minor inconveniences suffered by all ages, such as wars and political murders and mass hysteria, and personal fears and dreads and anxieties.

I am not defending the untenable position that there exist no differences in the spirit of one age as contrasted with another, or that certain historical epochs are not more or less stable than others. What I am suggesting is first, that the existence of "fixed principles" is a historical judgment not always so obvious to the actors at the time. To designate a style—Classical, Gothic, Baroque—is to signify the passing of an age. We know that it was a style, which is to say, that a certain distinct spirit suffused its chief institutions, its art, education, and politics, precisely because it has vanished from the earth and something "new" has arisen in its place. Second, and more important by far, I am suggesting that political theory has sprung less often from the urge to reflect "fixed principles" than from the impulse to meet the challenge actually to fix principles in the midst of what is seen by the aristocrat of the mind as chaos, or decline, stagnation, or suicidal destructiveness. By way of analogy, although the religious art of the high Middle Ages is customarily viewed as an expression of profound devotion, of unshakable faith, some of the greatest of such works might testify as well to the impulse of men of genius to assure themselves and others that God was indeed in His heaven, or even that there was a heaven at all. God *must* be in His heaven, else how could I have been inspired to sing His praises in my work: a touching, and superbly human, tautology. Art frequently arises from superfluity, agreed. But art may originate also in what the artist dares to acknowledge, however tacit the acknowledgement, as a lack. And so may political theory.

To explain more fully what I have in mind, I should like to turn formalist and to submit what sociologists of knowledge refer to as an "ideal" definition of politics. By politics I mean here that body of ideas, conventions, practices, institutions, and relationships directed toward carrying on the affairs of the public—in the absence of a knowable, definable, objective, immutable, transmittable common good. In the *absence* of something. That something is fixity, that something is certitude. Were the common good more surely accessible by means other than the political, there would then be no reason other than affection, or superstition perhaps, or aesthetic preference, for extending to politics a privileged position in the search. Politics begins with a lack: hence directives are needed, precepts discovered, deduced, or invented; political theories are created. If "fixed principles" ever truly existed, why the rage to express them? We would then possess something akin to political instincts and would require no special instruction. But if taking thought is a human substitute for natural instinct, or a supplement to it, then taking political thought must also be a substitute or supplement.

Political theory begins precisely at the moment when things become, so to speak, unglued. It is as if political thought from the beginning has exclaimed, however tacitly on occasion, "The civic god is dead, all is permitted," a challenge which becomes a democratic one only in the nineteenth century, when our rebellious intellectuals let the masses in on the Grand Inquisitor's dreadful secret— namely, that there *is* no secret. From the advent of political speculation, the unstated question seems to have gone something like this: "What will become of us, or rather what will they do to us—the rulers to the ruled, subjects to rulers, the many vulgar to the cultivated few, the privileged handful to the rank and file, common man to common man, even I to myself—in the absence of . . . what?" Personal authority, perhaps, or armed guards, or covenants, compacts, constitutions, codes of morality, systems of political education. No wonder Pascal could remark as he did upon the political thought of the ancient Greeks. If the ideal state appeared to have been designed for the governance of a madhouse, there was a reason. Only, the reason was left unstated by the likes of Plato and Aristotle.

In the absence of a set of precepts sufficient to import peace and unity into Italian life, Machiavelli designs in *The Prince* not a madhouse but, like Frederick II, a grand menagerie. The trainer must always be on his guard lest he be torn to pieces by the wild beasts of the political, while at the same time he must learn when to keep in check and when to release his own wild beast, his own stunning passion for power and dominion. All this to unify Italy or perhaps to solace his fellow Italians with the dazzling vision of the Italy that must surely one day rise from the ashes.

Hobbes designs not a zoo but a surgical facility, with no appeal beyond the Chief Physician. Here the beast is not tamed, he is dismembered. Hobbes' citizens become ambulatory basket cases, private consciences removed, arranged—and this is the horror of it—then learning how to arrange themselves for display in the activities wing. Come let us be citizens together; come let us be cripples together. To Hobbes, even that was preferable to internal division and perpetual warfare.

Rousseau designs not a ward for amputees but a citizen-army set in an encampment coextensive with the city. There they await battle, which ideally never comes. Only they do not know this. Their chief concern is to strengthen the collective body against the dread enemy. As good Spartans, they aid one another to purge themselves of impulses which sap the vitality of the whole: of particular interests, divisive doctrines, apparent wills. For this task what is wanted most is *esprit*. Soon the terrors of invasion fade even from their nocturnal dreams, and the life of the camp is sweetened by the achievement of collective morale. Rousseau alone, however, as the source of such solace, remains outside the camp as a recluse or enters occasionally, but then as a heartbroken non-believer.

In the view of political theory suggested here, modernity is no synonym for an absence of fixed principles, but is a term which combines the idea of democratic "disenchantment" with a determination not to emulate the absolutist systems of the past. Modernity is revolutionary in two senses: politically in the disclosure of the secret to us all—we know that the Emperor has no clothes; and philosophically in the resistance to substituting one metaphysical system for another. When he proclaimed that men would sooner have the void for their purpose than be void of purpose, Nietzsche thereby stated a proposition he hoped we might one day invalidate. By becoming aware of our insatiable craving for authority, both political and philosphical, we would be compelled to face up to our own sense of helplessness and consequent rage, that is, our resistance to coming of age. If we are witnessing the twilight of traditional political theory, it is because the aristocratic fathers are dead and we the children cannot, or will not, take that awful responsibility on ourselves, the care of the whole community. Instead, we see it as our job to fashion the theory and practice of our own discrete existence.

The task is as heroic for each who tries as it once was for the political theorist who strove in the name of the civil society, yet himself remained utterly alone, cut off from the solace whose mundane origins he recognized only too well. But the diffusion of heroism we now experience feels more like despair. Each and every one of us is expected somehow to become a system unto himself as well as a critic of that system, a city until himself as well as a dissident within its gates. If Kafka's Joseph K. is set adrift upon a fathomless sea, so in Plato's great novel is Glaucon. Only, in Socrates, Plato furnishes a rudder and a star, there to lead the fearful landsman safely ashore. But Kafka not only does not provide a benevolent Socrates, in his political dialogues he sends Joseph K. a pitiless counter-Socrates to plague his every lucid moment with mists and fogs and pitch blackness. That is, he sends to Joseph K.—just Joseph K. To qualify as a true modern, the democratic man is expected to compose his own script, he must think himself out of his predicament by himself. The rules do not permit him to call for the intervention of a foreign power. Even his therapist will deny his appeal for guiding principles having their origins outside himself, whether in philosophic systems, theological doctrines, or even psychological science itself.

It is we, the young and inexperienced, who are now to assume the burden which every past political theorist of stature, every aristocrat of the spirit, every paternal authority, had traditionally lived and suffered with. Those daring and incorrigible juveniles of the nineteenth century, Darwin and Freud, Kierkegaard, Nietzsche and the rest, would not be bought off, they were bound to divulge the secrets of the fathers. I see them dancing around the matrimonial bed, trembling with excitement at the prospect of broadcasting the news: ideas are not conceived in heaven after all. They perform their office as metaphysical spies and commandos, in order that all the children might be free, and in the extravagant conviction as well that some of us might even possess the strength to endure our freedom.

As a result, in neither his origins nor his destiny could Western man any longer regard himself as a privileged creature. Not only was he not privileged, he was rather the victim of the cruelest hoax nature could possibly play: he had been granted a consciousness that served only to make him more wretched. He was but a fly of summer and now he knew it. The disenchantment of the modern intellectual in the Western world would be furthered during the following century by such thinkers and artists as Weber and Russell and Heidegger, Joyce, and Beckett; by logical positivism, quantum mechanics, the Theater of the Absurd, by Dadaism and Freudianism. Liberation was the goal, smashing prison walls the chief preoccupation of the cultural vanguard. Wittgenstein described the prison as "A *picture* [which] held us captive. And we could not get outside it, for it lay in our language, and language seemed to repeat it to us inexorably." Free at last from the imprisoning conventions of our language, the twentieth-century playwright must take up and advance the work of Ibsen and Strindberg. His vocation, Ionesco says, is to "break up our language so that it can be put together again in order to re-establish contact . . . with multiple reality." By now, however, we may achieve so many perspectives—simultaneously—that we are compelled to hold fast lest we fly apart. Schoenberg in music, and Bohr and Heisenberg in physics, add still further "enlightenment."* And these are

---

*Heisenberg recalls that at Copenhagen in 1926 one question kept recurring to him and Niels Bohr: "Can nature possibly be as absurd as it seemed to us in these atomic experiments?" They finally persuaded themselves that it was, and that their interpretation led to a "complete, and, as many physicists believe, satisfactory solution of the situation." W. Heisenberg, *Physics and Philosophy* (1958), p. 42. The interpretation is complete and satisfactory, but only if one is willing to accept the rules, some of which, in the words of Andrade (1927), recall "irresistibly the teachings of the alchemists or the witches' kitchen in Faust." In J. C. Gregory, *A Short History of Atomism* (1931), p. 239.

but a few at the head of the list. Our language has been fractured, our metaphysics undermined, the very universe seems out of joint. If now to these upheavals in the realms of art, literature, science, philosophy, and social thought we add the political calamities of the past century, we may indeed see ourselves as living the crisis of modernity.

II

There was a long period during which nearly every thinking man was in some sense a rebel, and usually a quite irresponsible rebel. Literature was largely the literature of revolt or of disintegration. Gibbon, Voltaire, Rousseau, Shelley, Byron, Dickens, Stendhal, Samuel Butler, Ibsen, Zola, Flaubert, Shaw, Joyce—in one way or another they were all of them destroyers, wreckers, saboteurs. For two hundred years we had sawed and sawed and sawed at the branch we were sitting on. And in the end, much more suddenly than anyone had foreseen, our efforts were rewarded, and down we came. But unfortunately there had been a little mistake. The thing at the bottom was not a bed of roses after all, it was a cesspool full of barbed wire.

George Orwell, "Notes on the Way" (1940)

The first great political theories in the Western tradition were aimed at redressing a perilous imbalance within human beings and their societies. Socrates, perhaps the first of the remorseless questioners, might also have been the last. But there can be no doubt whatever that Plato is only the first, albeit the greatest, in a long line of political philosophers who sought less to increase than to answer the sum of critical questions confronting humanity. True, to read Plato in the spirit, say, of his *Phaedrus* is to put an end to believing that there were or ever could be definitive answers to such questions. But the Platonists and Neo-Platonists read the Master for the wisdom they saw contained within his "system," and that wisdom was located not so much in how Socrates went about the business of questioning, as in the substance of Platonic thought.

Though his aims were more modest, Aristotle contributed to the tradition of a politics of solace. He was not interested in man either as beast or as god—that is, in the frightening "aberrations" which often contort our souls—but in the creature who is "by nature a political animal" —a simple, brief definition of human nature eradicating all doubts. If we be "men," we have no choice other than to be "political." And to be political in a particular way, keeping at arm's length both beast and god within us and learning to accept the Golden Mean: Nothing too Much. No wonder so many of the Schoolmen would come to regard Aristotle as "almost a Christian," following in the footsteps of his Master, Plato. The point is that man is a moderate *by definition* rather than by experience. There is no distinction, as is made in Montaigne, between the person who chooses not to sin and the one who is incapable by nature of sinning.

The turbulent soul of Augustine produced in *The City of God* an engine of solace unmatched until the political philosophy of Aquinas. Yet Augustine's pages, like those of Plato, abound in examples of the skeptic responding with desperate power to his own profoundest doubts. The recognition that solace originates in their own troubled imaginations utterly cuts off both theorists from the comfort they provide their disciples. To cast a more ominous light on their predicament, we may also see them as creatures of monumental pride, apparently willing to live devoid of all solace. Despite the "heretical" nature of the teachings of Thomas Aquinas when viewed from the vantage point of our own time—and they were so viewed by the Church itself for the longest period—they usher in the great Age of Solace. From the vastnesses of the firmament to the minutest of God's creations, there is structure in the Universe, and Law both Natural and Divine.

But the human animal is restless, alternately bored and excited, an unmaker as well as a maker. The manifestations of these alternate states we call history. The structure of Christian solace is shattered by a Reformation in religion and a Renaissance in learning. Modern science waits in the wings to establish its own church upon the martyrdom of its founders. When it does make its appearance full-blown upon the stage of Western history it soon appears a threat to all traditional authority, secular as well as religious. The Age of the Enlightenment is a jeweler's glass held up to the facets of the cosmos, in the name of disenchantment, yet a new religion emerges upon the foundations of natural science. Not surprisingly, still another form of solace, remarkably similar to the forms which had preceded it, is granted Western humanity. There will be ample opportunity to examine the forms solace assumed in the Age of the Renaissance (Machiavelli), in the Age of Science (Hobbes), and in the Age of Enlightenment (Rousseau). For the present let up leap over those moments into modernity, where we were suspended at the end of the first part of the chapter.

The Age of Disenchantment, which is the nineteenth

century, committed the ultimate act of blasphemy. Down
came all religion, including the religion of Reason. And in
its wake, as if to mock the valiant blasphemers, came some
Liberation but far more tyranny, some equality but far
more cruelty, some respect for the human person but
much terror as well. For despite the dreams of the Liberators, the modern State had become the repository and
dispenser of solace. Movements demanding freedom and
justice would arise, in turn developing their own gifts of
solace, for the purpose either of keeping the fighters in the
ranks or of stilling the "triumphant" proletariat.

The choices seem clear: abhor the prideful act of grant-
ing solace, and accept ineffectuality; or embrace the dispensation of solace, without which "the masses" cannot
conceivably be moved, and become a monument to pride,
but effectual "in the world."

Those who choose the first course are rather special
cases, reflecting the cultural and metaphysical crisis of the
West in a unique manner, primarily aesthetic in character.
Resorting to the methods and magic of the Platos, Machiavellis, Hobbeses, and Rousseaus is unthinkable to them.
Yet the dispensation of solace has not gone unattended.
Even in the Anglo-American world, it has been undertaken
by a heartless and lawless nation-state and its leaders, before which the populace itself stands increasingly helpless.
And that is so not simply because of the overwhelming
power of the juggernaut.

The sapping of authority has inevitably been accompanied by a crisis in judgment, for centuries thought somehow linked to "common sense." But what today may be
regarded as "common" amongst men, even those occupy-

ing the same geographic boundaries and subject to the same laws and regulations? As for "sense," the doubts cast by science upon what was once believed to "make sense" have eroded the confidence of individuals and publics still further. Consequently, many of us cringe back from the precipice of judgment, for fear either of error or of fatal involvement in what we cannot even dimly comprehend. For such, political theory needs once again to become responsible, while somehow forsaking the mysteries accompanying the traditional sacraments of solace.

Ironically, those who feel the need for responsible theory simultaneously achieve, by that very recognition, both responsibility and impotence. But those who refuse to relinquish mystery and superstition—and their ranks include the overwhelming majority of intellectuals and political leaders throughout the world—continue successfully to offer solace on a vast scale. Theorists flourish who today still profess the doctrine that "truth" resides only in History, or in The Revolution; theorists abound who defend the dogma either of Western superiority or of Third World righteousness, and who condone torture and casual murder if need be in order to attain ends which they see as glorious, just, or foreordained.

Yet if one relinquishes recourse to the movements of solace, knowing only too well how often these movements are monstrously corrupted at their source by a pride which sets the solacer, like the Grand Inquisitor, contemptuously above the average run of humanity, what can one do save wash one's hands of the lot of it? One answer to this dilemma might arise from a reassessment of the relationship between pride and solace in political theory. The investigation of Machiavelli, Hobbes, and Rousseau may serve if not to fix that relationship, at least to permit us to hear variations on the theme by three of the greatest pre-nineteenth- century moderns. Only then might we attempt to come to grips with the terrible complexities of theorizing in our own time.

Chapter 2

Machiavelli's *Prince*:
The Political Actor
as Divine Instrument

Have you perchance seen ever in a field
What the behavior of an eagle is,
When fast and rage and hunger make her wild?
    And how she grabs a turtle, takes it up,
Then makes it fall to break its bony shell,
And then swoops down on its dead flesh to sup?
    Thus Fortune takes somebody to the spheres,
Oh, not to leave him there—to hurl him down,
So that she may enjoy his fall, his tears.
                Niccolò Machiavelli, "Fortune"

MACHIAVELLI'S *Prince* has been interpreted and appraised from a dazzling variety of perspectives. Responses have ranged from unqualified admiration for its refreshing candor to shock and outrage at what appears to some its strident immorality. *The Prince* has been condemned as a piece of political opportunism, an expression of the anti-Christ, and a work contributing to the political adventures of Napoleon, Mussolini, and Hitler. The Elizabethan dramatists enshrined Machiavelli's name in the literature as "Old Nick," still an alias for the Devil, and Shakespeare's audiences thrilled to the machinations of Iago and Richard III, trusting the playwright to bring the pair to justice in the end. *The Prince* has been acclaimed, on the other hand, not only as a forthright account of the spirit and practice of sixteenth-century Italian political life, but more recently as the first manifestation of a coherent science of politics and statecraft whose realism is that of modern times and whose intellectual courage is breathtaking. *The Prince* has now even been computerized and issued as a "guide to decision-making" for the use of "scholars and students as well as businessmen."*

Without disparaging most of these responses to the work, I should like to view *The Prince* from a different perspective, one which takes seriously Machiavelli's vision of the restoration of the wholeness of Italy: his quest for a Political Messiah whose will may be directed to the re-creation of the ancient virtues and glories of Rome; a Savior who will find his text not in Scripture, but in the inspired script which Machiavelli himself has prepared for his leading actor.

From this perspective *The Prince* is less an example of political science than an exercise in political alchemy. Suffering, despoliation, and ruin of every kind are to be transmuted into political grandeur. For what else is national

---

*Casyndekan Machiavelli, a Conceptual Index (Denver: Casyndekan, Inc., 1969). It is revealing of the treatment accorded the work that no author or editor is indicated. What a marvel, Machiavelli's *Prince* uncontaminated by humanity!

disintegration but a prelude to national rebirth? In an early chapter Machiavelli writes: "It was . . . necessary that Moses should find the people of Israel slaves in Egypt and oppressed by the Egyptians, so that they were disposed to follow him in order to escape from their servitude. It was necessary that Romulus should be unable to remain in Alba, and should have been exposed at his birth, in order that he might become King of Rome and founder of that nation. It was necessary that Cyrus should find the Persians discontented with the empire of the Medes, and the Medes weak and effeminate through long peace. Theseus could not have shown his abilities if he had not found the Athenians dispersed." All of the great founders—and legends —of the past had built upon adversity.

And in the concluding chapter Machiavelli says the same thing once again, only this time a crescendo is reached with a description of the plight of Italy, which measured by her suffering is a worthy addition to the congregation of Chosen Peoples: "And if, as I said, it was necessary in order that the power of Moses be displayed that the people of Israel should be slaves in Egypt, and to give scope for the greatness and courage of Cyrus that the Persians should be oppressed by the Medes, and to illustrate the pre-eminence of Theseus that the Athenians should be dispersed, so at the present time, in order that the might of an Italian genius might be recognized, it was necessary that Italy should be reduced to her present condition, and that she should be more enslaved than the Hebrews, more oppressed than the Persians, and more scattered than the Athenians; without a head, without order, beaten, despoiled, lacerated, and overrun, and that she should have suffered ruin of every kind." It is impossible to miss the grandeur of Machiavelli's dream: the greatest nations and their legendary heroes provide the materials for Machiavelli's imagination.

Note, moreover, that adversity is a "necessary," in fact, *indispensable*, prelude to greatness. As with nations, so also with men. Machiavelli himself had been beaten, Machiavelli himself had been despoiled, lacerated, had suffered ruin of every kind. But he shall yet prevail. I suppose that is what men mean when they speak of making a virtue of necessity. The only alternative for Machiavelli, as for Italy, was simply to submit to fate, to accept defeat and renounce all visions of future glory, a strategy not likely to commend itself to the Renaissance temperament. Machiavelli anticipates the day when both he and his beloved Italy would get back their own. "When the bright Spring returns, open and bold," goes one of the greatest of Machiavelli's poems,

> And chases winter from our earth away, —
> A foe to ice and snow and to the cold,

> Then Heaven shows its most benevolent face,
> And with her train of Nymphs Diana comes
> Back to our woods for her accustomed chase;

> And the day seems more clear and beautiful,
> Especially if the sun comes up to shine
> Between both horns of the celestial bull.*

---

*"The Golden Ass," an unfinished work after Apuleius, which has the poet, transformed into an ass, observe and ridicule others who had been transformed into beasts by his guide, Circe.

Spring will come again, even to old Machiavelli—historian, poet, playwright, prodigious writer of letters, diplomat and organizer of militias—even to Machiavelli now stripped of his career by a change of political seasons and made to fear for his life. "It is rather a miracle I am alive," he wrote a nephew in 1513, at the very time he was revising *The Prince*, "because my office has been taken from me and I have been on the point of losing my life, which God and my innocence have saved for me. I have endured all sorts of evils, both of prison and other things. Yet by the grace of God I am well, and I manage to live as I can and so I'll try to do, until the heavens show themselves more favorable." A man's fate is not his character alone; Fortune has much to do with it.

As with Machiavelli, so with Florence, and with Italy as well: she must nourish the conviction that one day the heavens will indeed show themselves more favorable. *The Prince* is Machiavelli's salve for her wounded pride. Once upon a time Rome had been the glory of the universe; then her star was eclipsed. But she is destined to rise again, to even greater heights of glory, led by a political hero coached by Niccolò Machiavelli in the arts of conquest, a composite of Moses and Cyrus, Theseus and Romulus. "And it is," begins a later stanza of his poem, "and always will be, and was

> Always so: evil follows good; good evil;
> And each is of the other the sole cause.

Each is of the other the sole cause. The ruthless Prince, that royal pirate and worse, that great thing of evil, will yet sow the seed of goodness, the flower of a new Rome. And were it not for adversity, were not Machiavelli disgraced and exiled from Florence, what then of Old Nick himself? Would there have been *The Prince* and *The Discourses*, the sprightly plays, the histories, the poems, the beautiful letters? Were it not for adversity, would the world have been enriched by the joy of his works and his memory? No one can say for sure.* But there does appear an alchemy at work in the human soul, a curious magic: adversity "becomes" greatness; greatness always "turns" at the last to ashes. And each of the other the sole cause? Who can tell.

We know only this: in his exile Machiavelli wished that "the present Medici lords"— those who had retaken Florence, banished the Republic, and exiled Machiavelli— "will make use of me, even if they begin by making me roll a stone." Even the employment of Sisyphus, provided only it be in the world, even such employment is preferable to a life outside the city. But it was denied him almost to the last, so what else was poor Machiavelli to do but write?

I

I love my native city more than my own soul.
                                Niccolò Machiavelli

---

*Any more than one can state with complete assurance that the adversity suffered by such accomplished men of action as Thucydides, Napoleon, or Trotsky was not responsible (in the sense of providing the occasion, as well as the motivation) for producing their powerful writings. But we *do* know that one of the most dazzling passages in all of Machiavelli's prose appears in *The Art of War*, where he is straining in exile to blot from all memory his humiliating defeat at Prato, by fighting the battle all over again—this time *in words*. It is not necessary to say which side wins.

We, who no longer take for granted the immortality
of the soul, are apt to overlook the poignance of
Machiavelli's credo. At the time he wrote, the
expression was no cliche but meant literally that
one was prepared to forfeit an everlasting life or to
risk the punishments of hell for the sake of the city.
The question, as Machiavelli saw it, was not whether
one loved God more than the world, but whether
one was capable of loving the world more than
one's own self.

Hannah Arendt

Machiavelli's message in *The Prince,* viewed as a vision
of Italy restored to wholeness, seems a secular paraphrase
of the national incantation of the ancient Hebrews, this time
addressed to the Hero rather than to the Folk. "Hear, O
Prince, the God our Nation, the God is One." For Italy
actually to become One, a new man must be made to appear
in the world. That new man is Machiavelli's superb artistic
creation, the Prince. Like Moses, the Prince is to be the
lieutenant of the Idea on earth, the implacable bearer of the
Word. He is to be the prophet, armed with Machiavelli's
Idea. Machiavelli summons his lieutenant to the Burning
Bush. Following the Overture, the summons appears at the
beginning, in the strings, gently, and is thundered again in
the Finale. But the summons to the holy place is at once also
a summons to the Mount of Revelation. For Machiavelli's
gift is likewise the Tables, a new Law couched in a new language of politics. Machiavelli couples imitation of the legendary heroes of the past with bold action to create a new
political art. This new art is utterly devoid of content, its
teaching precisely the opposite of "Be yourself." Its precept is, instead, "Be your *roles.*" The object is to create a

man of a thousand faces, a master performer who eventually does become his roles.

Although Machiavelli is most generally interpreted as a scientist owing, I imagine, to the "naturalism" of his political vocabulary,* the method he himself sets forth in the Dedicatory Letter to *The Prince* is the method of the artist. Unlike those who assume a fixed position and relentlessly press the inquiry, Machiavelli continually shifts position to cultivate the eye of the artist. His aphoristic writing shows greater concern for a multiplicity of perspectives than for any fixed order. In the "same way that landscape painters station themselves in the valleys in order to draw mountains or high ground," he writes, "and assume an eminence in order to get a good view of the plains, so it is necessary to be a prince to know thoroughly the nature of the people, and one of the populace to know the nature of princes."

Yet Machiavelli himself is no Prince; neither is he a commoner. He is something else, something more, something entirely new as the Renaissance was new, something which permits him to be neither and both at one and the same time. Machiavelli is the most skillful of all manipulators of the lives of others, the political playwright. How

---

*See Harold D. Lasswell and Abraham Kaplan, *Power and Society* (1950), p. 118, n. 15: "A rough classification of a sample of 300 sentences from each of the following [political theorists] yielded these proportions of political philosophy (demand statements and valuations) to political science (statements of fact and empirical hypotheses): Aristotle's *Politics*, 25 to 75; Rousseau's *Social Contract*, 45 to 55; Laski's *Grammar* [*of Politics*], 20 to 80. Machiavelli's *Prince*, by contrast, *consisted entirely (in the sample) of statements of political science in the present sense.*" (My emphasis.) I wonder how our authors view Chapter XXVI, the concluding chapter, which is entitled "Exhortation to Liberate Italy from the Barbarians," and closes with a quotation from that immortal empiricist, Petrarch.

better to achieve perspective, to "know" a Prince for example, than to write oneself into his role? All Italy is a stage
and every Italian an actor; the victory goes always to the
most accomplished player.

The Romans, Machiavelli tells us, had bestowed the
consulate upon "those who best knew how to entertain the
people, and not [upon] . . . those who best knew how to
conquer their enemies." Certainly this is a sign of corruption, but is there reason to assume less corruption in Machiavelli's Italy? He himself was never guilty of that extravagance. The "great majority of mankind are satisfied with
appearances," he wrote, "as though they were realities,
and are often more influenced by the things that seem,
than by those that are."

The preoccupation of *The Prince* is with new princi-
palities, new monarchies, new dominions—*and* with things
that seem. The new state calls for the new man, the new
performer, the Prince who does not inherit but first acquires and then re-creates the state. Force might prove
useful in ruling an established state. Acting is what is most
required to found a new one. "I believe it to be the most
true that it seldom happens that men rise from low condition to high rank without employing either force or
fraud. . . . Nor do I believe that force alone will ever be
found to suffice, whilst it will often be the case that cunning
alone serves the purpose. . . . Nor do I believe that there
was ever a man who from obscure condition arrived at great
power by merely employing open force; but there are
many who have succeeded by fraud alone." They are obliged
to simulate "until they have become powerful enough so
that force alone suffices them." With Xenophon, Machia-

velli honors the precept that "a prince who wishes to achieve great things must learn to deceive."

Now, this might pose a certain difficulty: how may one *learn* to deceive? Machiavelli has an answer. "Let no one marvel if in speaking of new dominions both as to prince and state, I bring forward very exalted instances, for men walk almost always in the paths trodden by others, proceeding in their actions by imitation." Ability is identified with the successful imitation of heroes like Cyrus and Hiero, Caesar, Brutus, Romulus, and Theseus.

At this point, still near the beginning of *The Prince*, Machiavelli does what at first appears a rather curious thing. He takes great pains to suggest and to elaborate the idea of Moses as Prince—the Moses who was, after all, not just any run-of-the-mill political genius, but the anointed of God. The "fact of a private individual becoming a prince presupposes either great ability or good fortune. . . .

Nevertheless those who have been less beholden to good fortune have maintained themselves best. . . . But to come to those who have become princes through their own merits and not by fortune, I regard as the greatest, Moses, Cyrus, Romulus, Theseus, and their like. And although one should not speak of Moses, he having merely carried out what was ordered by God, still he deserves admiration, if only for the grace which made him worthy to speak with God. But regarding Cyrus and others who have acquired or founded kingdoms, they will all be found worthy of admiration; and if their particular actions and methods are examined they will

not appear very different from those of Moses, although he had so great a master.

Moses had the greatest of Masters, the others obviously
lesser ones. But Machiavelli adds that "in examining their
life and deeds it will be seen that they owed nothing to
fortune but the opportunity which gave them matter to be
shaped into what form they thought fit [The analogy once
again to the artist, this time to the sculptor] and without
that opportunity their powers would have been wasted,
and without their powers the opportunity would have come
in vain."

In my understanding of the relevant passages, Machiavelli introduces Moses for at least two purposes: in order
to launch a discussion of the relation of individual *virtu* to
national fate; and to impress upon the apprentice Prince
the enormous advantage of a "script," one preferably composed by a master playwright. Moses had so great a Master. Fortunate indeed is Lorenzo, who has his master in
Machiavelli.*

Moses the playwright, after forty days and nights upon
the Mount of Revelation, where he is coached in the composition of the Tables, descends to the community, there
in turn to direct his own Prince, Aaron, in the reading of
his lines. Moses's inspiration had been the search for God,
and the dream of a nation of warriors wrought from a de-
jected multitude of slaves. The god of Machiavelli is his

---

*Some of Machiavelli's compatriots thought along similar lines. Filippo da
Casavecchia wrote to his friend Niccolò upon the occasion of the fall of Pisa, June
8, 1509, to a militia recruited and organized by Machiavelli: "I see more clearly
that you are the greatest prophet the Jews or any other people ever had."

divine vision of what Italy might one day become, his
Tables the manual prepared under the direction of the
muse of History, like the Tables of Moses shaped in the
wasteland, in exile from his people.

The grace possessed by Moses could have been nothing
other than Moses's own ability. Those who had "become
princes through their own merits and not by fortune"—
Moses, Cyrus, and the rest—Machiavelli regards "as the
greatest." Why should Moses be placed at the head of the
list, unless his merit *was* his grace? "And although one
should not speak of Moses . . . still he deserves admiration,
if only for that grace which made him worthy to speak with
God." Now it seems plain that Machiavelli wishes very
much to speak of Moses. And it also seems plain that he
identifies the grace of Moses with Moses's "own merit,"
the grace which made him worthy of accepting direction
from God. The merit of Moses consisted in this: the recognition of God, the composition of the script according to
the will of God, and the determination, come what may,
to effectuate God's will in the world, as set forth in the
Tables. Now there is dedication, there is majesty!

Moses possessed the amplitude of soul to recognize fate
and the genius to make himself her accomplice. All leaders
must become the accomplices of Fortune, and not her adversaries. For what else is Fortune than the inscrutable
will of Heaven? In *The Discourses* Machiavelli makes the
identification explicit. "I repeat, then, as an incontrovert-
ible truth, proved by all history, that men may second
Fortune, but cannot oppose her; they may develop her
designs, but cannot defeat them." Those who have rebelled
have been ruthlessly eliminated. Fortune often blinds men.

When she wishes to "effect the ruin and destruction of states, she places men at the head who contribute to and hasten such ruin; and if there be anyone powerful enough to resist her, she has him killed, or deprives him of all means of doing any good." Which, after all, was the fate even of Moses, when he lost his steadfastness.

Yet Machiavelli concludes this very discussion, this fear and trembling before the Powers That Be, this mournful poem, this dirge to the impotence of man, with these wild words: "But men should never despair on that account; for, not knowing the aims of Fortune, which she pursues by dark and devious ways, men should always be hopeful, and never yield to despair, whatever troubles or ill fortune may befall them." Even if they be the troubles of a Job.* Can these be the words of a rational observer of human affairs, the intellectual hero to a whole race of social scientists, or are they the words of a madman, a fanatic or, worse yet, a poet? Men cannot defeat Fortune, cannot control their destinies unaided. Still, never despair—courage, brother, courage.

What rescues Machiavelli's exhortation and renders it less fanciful is the political context in which it was written. Italy *was* suffering, Italy *was* destitute, Italy *was* being hacked to pieces. And that happens to *all* peoples, in *all* places, throughout the major portions of their histories: read the Old Testament, reflect upon the fate of the Athens of Theseus, the Persia of Cyrus, or the Rome of the Caesars. So the sufferings of the Italian people were not caused

---

*In his poem "Fortune," Machiavelli writes: "So, let us grab her as she turns and shines,/ And, as much as we can, at every hour,/ Adjust ourselves to all her whims and signs."

by some unique flaw in themselves; what was required was not private therapy, aimed at overcoming character disorders, but *public, heroic action*. Instead of dwelling upon present miseries, and attempting to *explain* them, consider the immortals—not the political philosophers full of noble and pretentious sentiments, but the great political actors —and learn from them the arts of reformation and founding. All the while, think upon the glory and fame, the ecstasies, which await the shining deliverer of Italy.

After acknowledging some of the difficulties and shedding a glimmer of hope, Machiavelli will set forth to entice his Prince with promises of joy everlasting. That seduction is the most cunning and inventive aspect of the political art of Machiavelli.

II

[Machiavelli's] political works have lived because they too are works of art, and, in their less flexible way, were subject to the same creative, shaping pressures as were his literary works. The way in which a thing is said is part of its meaning, and in assessing the judgments of a writer on politics, and considering his arguments, his emphases, and his use of evidence—if that man was also the greatest dramatist of his age, would it not be prudent to keep that fact in mind?

J. R. Hale

Someone once inquired of Demosthenes, "What is the chief part of an orator?" "Acting," replied Demosthenes. "What next?" "Acting." "What next again?" "Acting!" It might seem curious that what is generally considered superficial in an orator, at least when compared with the substance of his address, and which is actually the craft of the playactor, should be of such importance to the greatest orator of them all—that it should in fact be the one indispensable virtue. On reflection the reason becomes plain enough. Or at any rate, so Demosthenes reasoned. There is in each of us a good deal more of the fool than there is of the wise man; therefore those faculties by which the foolish part of ourselves is captivated are the most effective. And the foolish part is most reliably captivated by acting. Were we to inquire of Machiavelli the chief part of his Prince, we would receive the identical reply: acting. For Machiavelli gives little instruction in how to treat wisdom in the victims of the Prince, but much instruction in how to exploit foolishness.

In *The Prince* political art is the capacity of the unique man to transmute words and events into *appearance*. Political ability is above all the ability to fashion an accomplice worthy of gaining the ear of Fortune, even as Moses on occasion instructed God. Machiavelli writes that "he errs least and will be most favored by fortune who suits his proceedings to the times." But suiting one's proceedings to the times rather than to one's natural inclinations is a difficult art to master. Nor will fashioning a single character, however skillfully conceived, suffice. The repertoire of the Prince must be marvelously versatile. After all, the actor who scores a smashing success as Lear, then attempts to play Henry V as Lear and Prospero as Lear and even Abe Lincoln in Illinois as Lear, cuts a ridiculous figure. He has become as specialized as the dinosaur. Not only will rules differ, but roles as well.

The successful Prince must be a master at adapting himself to new rules and new roles. Take the case of Hiero of Syracuse, who attained to the Princehood from private life. Hiero had enjoyed a unique reputation for virtue while still a private citizen; upon becoming the embodiment of political authority, however, he "abandoned his old friendships and formed others," he "abolished the old militia" and "raised a new one." That is, he cashed in the chips of private virtue for a new sort of credit. He adapted to the changed circumstances of his life, no longer the friend but the public man. Hiero began to act.

Elsewhere Machiavelli tells us the story of Appius Claudius, by nature a vicious and tyrannical person. Appius had laid a careful campaign against the people of Rome to make himself their sole master. He also commenced to act, becoming so popular with the multitude that "it seemed a wonder how he could in so short a time, have acquired, as it were, a new nature and a new spirit, having until then been regarded as a cruel persecutor of the people." Once he had achieved his goal, however, Appius promptly dropped the act "and began to display his innate arrogance," abandoning the theater for the prison and the gallows. Alas, his sense of timing had deserted him, which is fatal even to the most accomplished of performers. He changed "too suddenly from one quality to the extreme opposite. . . . Although his astuteness in deceiving the people by simulating their party was well employed," yet it was "very ill-judged in him suddenly to change his character. . . —from being humane to become haughty, and from being easy of access to become difficult—and to do this so suddenly and without excuse that everybody could see the falseness of his soul. For he who for a time has seemed good, and for purposes of his own wants to become bad, should do it gradually, and should seem to be brought to it by the force of circumstance. . . . Otherwise his deception will be discovered, and he will . . . be ruined." The reason that Machiavelli's leading player, Cesare Borgia, literally the Valentino of Italy (he was Duke of Valentine), conquered was because "He dissembled . . . so well."

Now an Appius, a Borgia, must appear good for a time. But consider: to succeed, Hiero, by nature good, must on occasion appear bad. Which is the more demanding role, being bad and appearing good, or being good and appearing bad? On reflection, it would seem more difficult for a decent and honorable man to pretend evil than for an evil one to feign virtue. To appear good Appius has but to spare a villain or two; to appear bad Hiero must on occasion disembowel a saint. If he reverts to his true character, will Hiero be any less vulnerable than Appius? But there is even more to it than that. Machiavelli is further persuaded that in politics a "man who wishes to make a profession of goodness in everything must necessarily come to grief among so many who are bad." For most, then, mastering oneself involves not so much the struggle to become good, which is the construction Christian custom placed upon this striving, as it does the struggle to become bad, should the situation demand it. The Prince must learn the capacity for wickedness by subduing whatever impulses to compassion, friendship, or honor stir within him.

The goal for Machiavelli's political warrior is pure artifice, pure invention, a thousand masks without the man

behind them. And the best way of acquiring the skills of
the chameleon is by imitation: there is no substitute for
apprenticeship. The Prince "ought to read history and
study the actions of eminent men, see how they acted in
warfare, examine the causes of their victories and defeats
in order to imitate the former and avoid the latter, and
above all, do as some men have in the past, who have imitated some one, who has been much praised and glorified,
and have always kept his deeds and actions before them,
as they say Alexander the Great imitated Achilles, Caesar
Alexander, and Scipio Cyrus." For his part, Machiavelli
has learned one basic and useful truth from a study of the
acts of *all* great men, a single axiom upon which the political art may be said to rest: the *"one who deceives will
always find those who allow themselves to be deceived."*
Art will find its audience. The art of politics is the art of
seduction, nothing less than the "astuteness to confuse
men's brains."

Rulers are to be conquered by the arts of war—one
plays the lion with one's peers. The "chief cause of the loss
of states" Machiavelli believed to be the Prince's neglect
of the arts of war. But subjects are captivated and held enthralled by the arts of theater—by the fox playing either
the lion or the lamb, but never on any account the fox for
all to see.

Machiavelli urges his Prince to accept the stage setting.
He must not delude himself as to the mood of the audience. If public taste itself is corrupt, the Prince "must follow its humor and satisfy it." But under no circumstances
must he permit others—persent company excepted of

course—to compose the script. Princes ought to "avoid as much as possible being under the will and pleasure of others." Natural, and sometimes even conventional limits upon action must be acknowledged in practice, but never the wills of other men, for then the Prince is defenseless against them and is surely doomed. Why seek the advice of others when "men will always be false . . . unless compelled by necessity to be true"? "Only those defenses are good, certain, and durable, which depend on yourself alone and your own ability." To persuade the Prince, it remains only for Machiavelli to link his brilliant consideration of Fortune and ability with the destinies of Italy.

The link is made by the mediary term *she*. Fortune is a "woman": "you wish to master her"; "she lets herself be overcome"; "she is always a friend to the young." But then so is Italy a woman: Machiavelli speaks of "her redemption"; "she awaits one who may heal her wounds"; "she prays God to send some one to redeem her." Italy is the prostrate Madonna, ravished by foreigners, even by her own sons. The suffering but still fertile body of Italy is to be delivered by a consummate political actor, who will be delivered, in turn, by Machiavelli the theorist.

Were Machiavelli a Spaniard, how the pageantry of the *corrida* would have suited him: the fierce sun of passion, the yellow sand, the flourishes, the excitement of the crowd, the stark power of the bull, the cold fury of the sword; but before that the sinuous dance, the mastery of the matador; throughout, the dark, veiled feminine beauty, the suggestively thrown blood-rose. But as we know, matadors seldom die in bed. Machiavelli knew that. But he also knew something else far more chilling. In Italy, as in most civilized nations, it is not always so easy to tell the matador from the bull.

III

For some time I have never said what I believed, and never believed what I said, and if I do sometimes happen to say what I think, I always hide it among so many lies that it is hard to recover.

Niccolò Machiavelli, Letter to Guicciardini

Fortune is a Woman. If you wish to master her you must be bold. Meanwhile she—this time the "she" has become Italy—awaits her lover and her redeemer. But if Italy is to be redeemed, then Machiavelli himself must also master the feminine arts, at least as he conceives them in his imagination. He must also become a woman: not the passive, long-suffering creature he portrays as Italy, but an active, wily siren with an empty womb and an irresistible call. He must seduce his Prince, entice him with visions of sugarplums—power and glory and the love of women, and all that. He must, like some brilliant and determined woman, entertain the Prince with promised ecstasies while directing the outcome of his pleasure-seeking activities to serve the needs of the nation. The Prince is flattered as a lover: he is to be used by Machiavelli to father a State. Machiavelli will direct the raging passions of his Prince to this noblest of political ends.

By his rhetorical wiles Machiavelli will beguile the Man

Who Acts into undertaking the outrageous course which the salvation of Italy demands. But he will at the same time conceal from the Prince that it is he, Machiavelli, and not the Prince who leads. The Prince is to be an instrument in the hands of the political theorist; but to the man of action it must always appear that the man of words is but an instrument which exists for the gratification of his own political lusts.

In his delightful play, *Mandragola*, Machiavelli has an elderly magician use an ardent young lover much as Machiavelli would use his Prince. The young man cannot rest until he has gained the bed of a beautiful woman, wife to a respectable but impotent old fool. The young blade's appetite is only made keener by the perils of the adventure. By his superior knowledge of human nature, and his superb timing, the sorcerer manages to deceive every character in the play, save the clever serving-man of the love-starved youth, himself an experienced spectator of the foibles of others. He deceives the husband who desires an heir, the corrupt friar who desires a contribution to the Church, the lover who desires an evening's pleasure, the young wife who has never truly tasted love. He demonstrates with surpassing brilliance how it is possible, by deception alone, to have everyone derive some benefit to himself. That the scheme works illustrates the principle upon which Shakespeare's great "Machiavellian" creature, Richard III, acquires a throne: everyone is delighted to *be* deceived.

In Machiavelli's play what *seems* is constantly confused with what *is*, individual gratifications with institutional requisites: the appetites of the young lover with the needs of the childless family; the venality of the friar with the welfare of the Church; the eroticism of the young pair with the continuation, if not of the species, then at least of the family name, most certainly of the family estate. The lover delivers his lady from dull and sterile bondage, and presumably she conceives. Similarly, Italian interests are to be served by the theorist directing the virile appetites of the man of action.

Now, the estate of Machiavelli's Prince is sheer fantasy.* But then, so is the estate of perpetual lover, the perpetual imp of sensuous joy; and how many Lotharios would give up the fantasy for the reality? It is this blindly determined preference which permits the magician, and the political theorist, to do their work in the world. To revert to an earlier figure: for the scheme to succeed, the man of action must never for a moment doubt that he is the matador. But by directing his passions with consummate skill, Machiavelli hopes to cast him in a rather different role. Whether he knows it or not, the would-be Prince, poor chap, is the bull.

Unlike *Mandragola, The Prince* is not farce but melancholy farce, not comedy but tragi-comedy. For its hero is doomed, as remorselessly as nature dooms any creature she has done using. And as theorist Machiavelli resembles a force of nature. There he stands, back of the barrier, honing the sacrificial blade, reassuring his Prince with a Chap-

---

*To his friend Vettori he wrote: "[I] have composed a little work *On Princedoms*. . . . If ever you can find any of my fantasies pleasing, this one should not displease you; and by a prince, and especially by a new prince, it ought to be welcomed."

linesque grin, innocent, beguiling and perhaps the least bit roguish.

Machiavelli pretends to be sharpening the sword for his matador-Prince, who will win glory, fame, power, riches, and the love of women, while the multitude shouts his praises. If only the Prince will permit Machiavelli to instruct him in the arts of the contest. All Machiavelli's Prince has to do to achieve what the master calls "felicity" is to divest himself of his deepest nature and become an artifact. He has merely to make himself into a mask. Machiavelli concocts a devil's pact, and for him the stakes are the highest: the salvation of his beloved Italy. Could the devil's pact which Machiavelli is customarily accused of having offered against the people in fact be one skillfully drawn against the Prince himself?

All the Prince has to do is to become an invention instead of a person, to purge himself of his former beliefs, his former passions, his friends—if any—his enemies, his hatreds, to become a work of the highest Renaissance art. There is a horrible fascination in witnessing the ways men have of preparing others for the sacrifice. To my mind, the Prince is intended as nothing less than a sacrifice offered up to heal the bleeding wounds of Italy. Witness the words with which Machiavelli concludes *The Prince*: "This opportunity must not," he exhorts Lorenzo, or some potential Lorenzo, "be allowed to pass, so that Italy may at length find her liberator. I cannot express the love with which he would be received in all those provinces which have suffered under these foreign invasions, with what thirst for vengeance, with what steadfast faith, with what love, with what grateful tears. What doors would be closed against

him? What people would refuse him obedience? What
envy could oppose him? What Italian would withold
allegiance?"

Yet when he is done with the founder, Machiavelli will
cast him aside, without remorse, in favor of ordered politics
and legitimate government. That is, Machiavelli knows
that the Italian people, once unified, will eventually establish such a politics and such a government. *The Prince* ex-
tends an invitation to the founder; *The Discourses* instruct
the citizens in the maintenance of an ordered society. And
in *The Discourses* the citizens are urged to kill the founder
of their nation if that is necessary to save it.

The lamb is to be convinced that he may successfully
play the lion. He is adorned with garlands, anointed and
blessed, then sent out as a brilliant art-work to perform the
role of Hero. He is no hero but a fiction. Are all heroes
works of fiction?

Even as Machiavelli rehearses the powers and the glories, the joys and endless delights which await the Prince,
he hones the blade. For the Prince is but a stop-gap, a
transition between chaos and stable government, a sort of
one-man proletariat necessary to usher in the new order.
The moment he succeeds in unifying and pacifying Italy,
the Prince will vanish by the logic of his very function. *It
will be the first legitimate act of the Republic to murder its
founder*. Legitimate because necessary. For the gravest
threat to the nation itself can then come only from the un-
bridled ambition of the Hero. The very qualities required
for creating the state prevent the Prince from taking his
place in a peaceful political community. Machiavelli was
familiar with the practice of the ancients who either mur-

dered or exiled their founders. Prudence demanded as much.

"The welfare . . . of a republic or a kingdom," Machiavelli wrote, "does not consist in having a prince who governs it wisely during his lifetime, but in having one who will give it such laws that it will maintain itself even after his death." Machiavelli condones the murder of Remus by Romulus and, more significantly, the murder of his own sons by Brutus, on the ground that such actions were necessary. "To Preserve the Newly Recovered Liberty in Rome, It Was Necessary That the Sons of Brutus Should Have Been Executed" is the title of Chapter III, Book III of *The Discourses*. "And whoever makes himself tyrant of a state and does not kill Brutus, or whoever restores liberty to a state and does not immolate his sons, will not maintain himself in his position long." For Machiavelli the spectacle of Junius Brutus immolating his own flesh and blood is one of the sublimest episodes in the history of politics. "The severity of Brutus was not only useful, but necessary for the maintenance of that liberty which he had restored to her; and certainly it is one of the rarest examples within the memory of man for a father not only to sit in judgment and condemn his own sons, but actually to be present at their execution."

You wish to be a Prince? Good, then you must be prepared, if necessary, to immolate your own sons. You wish to be a founder? Fine. Lead your own Isaac to the mountain.

By the same logic, whichever citizens of a stable state will not kill the Hero-Prince—that raging Don Juan of power and pride—once he has assured stability and is himself the gravest threat to stability, will surely lose their liberties, and most likely their lives as well. The Prince in Machiavelli's scheme is a deadman, a much glorified deadman, a regal deadman even, but a corpse nevertheless.

In the same century which witnessed the publication of *The Prince*, Francis Bacon, another gifted man of words disappointed in his infatuation with political power and formally disqualified for public office, wrote a remarkable little essay called "Of Great Place." In the measure to which Machiavelli's work sought to encourage a Prince, Bacon's laid bare the supreme folly of political ambition. "Men in great place," he wrote,

> are thrice servants: servants of the sovereign or state, servants of fame, and servants of business; so they have no freedom, neither in their persons nor in their actions nor in their times. It is a strange desire, to seek power and to lose liberty; or to seek power over others and to lose power over a man's self. The rising unto place is laborious, and by pains men come to greater pains; and it is sometimes base, and by indignities men come to dignities. The standing is slippery, and the regress is either a downfall or at least an eclipse, which is a melancholy thing. . . . Certainly great persons had need to borrow other men's opinions to think themselves happy, for if they judge by their own feeling they cannot find it; but if they think with themselves what other men think of them and that other men would fain be as they are, then they are happy as it were by report, when perhaps they find the contrary within. For they are the first that find their

own griefs, though they be the last that find their
own faults. Certainly men in great fortunes are
strangers to themselves, and . . . Death presses
heavily on the man who is known to all others but
dies ignorant of himself.

Now, Machiavelli knew all that. Had *he* not been
brought down, was *he* not alone, suffering devastation in
the wilderness, the taste of ashes in his mouth? Employing
a form not likely to commend itself to the attention of the
busy man of action—in his poem "Ingratitude"—had
Machiavelli not himself demonstrated equal mastery of
the kind of lament unleashed by Francis Bacon? He writes
there that for having served, political men are customarily
rewarded for their efforts

With both a wretched life and violent death.

Therefore, since foul Ingratitude still lives,
Let everyone abhor both court and state:

For there's no shorter way to make man hate
The things he wanted most, once he has had them.

So Machiavelli knew, all right. Then why did he not
speak out, why did he not tell his Prince the harsh truths
attendant upon the lusting after political power? Why did
not Machiavelli instruct him in the sham and emptiness of
his public role, and the bitterness of his inevitable fall? The
only answer I find convincing, the only sense made by the
publication of *The Prince* at all, is that Machiavelli intended
not to enlighten the politically ambitious man, but to se-

duce him into undertaking heroic, even preposterous, deeds because such deeds were required for the redemption of Italy.

Machiavelli's Prince will be happy only by report, but Machiavelli does not tell him this. He will come to pains and to greater pains still in his ruthless climb to the top of the heap, but Machiavelli does not tell him this. Death will press heavily upon him, for he will indeed die ignorant of himself. In fact, he will have no self at all, being a work of art, all surface and no depth. Michelangelo fashioned no entrails for his statues; neither did Machiavelli for his Prince.

The Prince is created by divesting human nature of its humanity. It dies when its functions have become obsolete or else threatening. Yet there is a certain justification for Machiavelli's refusal to disclose the full story to the Prince. There is, after all, none so blind as will not see. Such a one is the man of monumental political ambitions. The Prince has no thoughts of his own death because he is no longer truly among the living. The Prince himself is always his first victim: he must assassinate himself, whatever selfhood he might ever have possessed, to protect against his own, inevitable, assassination. Such a political man must make himself his first victim for still another reason: after the first crime, killing comes easy. Is not that first crime a moral suicide?

Machiavelli celebrates the powers and the glories of his Prince, and whets the sword. Then he hands it to the victim and beckons him to the center of the ring. To the roars of a frenzied and grateful populace, the Prince slays the great black bull, the terrible beast of chaos and random violence, of wars of rivalry and petty jealousy, the monster that had ravaged Italy for over a millenium. Then, much to the astonishment of the triumphant Prince, Machiavelli takes the blade from him and plunges it into his breast. *Consummatum est*: the Deed is done; Italy is saved.

Such, of course, is almost always the script composed by the theorist for his "instrument." Let us set the stage once again and this time have political "reality" direct the action.

Machiavelli celebrates the powers and glories of his Prince, and whets the sword. Then he hands it to the intended victim and beckons him to the center of the ring. Quite ominously the crowd has vanished. The Prince has his way with the great black bull, the clumsy beast of constraint and limitation, of laws and regulations, checks of every kind upon the ambitions of the Prince. Then, much to the astonishment of the triumphant Machiavelli, whose Prince had actually succeeded in acquiring power by his plan, after the ritual slaying the matador plunges the blade into the breast of the Master. *Consummatum est*: the Deed is done; the political ambitions of a new Prince are unleashed upon the unhappy land. For it is frequently seen as a necessity by the tyrant to murder his own tutor. Nero must insist upon the suicide of Seneca. Should the plan of the theorist fail, off with his head; should it succeed against enormous odds, the new ruler needs no "conscience." Besides, the man of action will share his glory with no other mortal.

Yet Machiavelli was almost surely fated to die in bed. His scheme was so grandiose, so utopian in character, set so far in the future, that retribution would be impossible. In fact, the unification of the Italian peninsula was not accomplished until three hundred years after the death of Machiavelli. But if the plan itself did not succeed in the sixteenth century, the vision of a unified Italy glowed in Machiavelli's writings, a solace to literate Italians for ten generations.

Chapter 3

Behold *Leviathan*!:
The Systematic Solace
Of Thomas Hobbes

IN the Book of Job, from whose verses Thomas Hobbes borrowed the title for his great work on politics, man has God by the beard and is bent upon extorting from Him answers to his pain, his lonliness, and his defeat. God the Creator turns upon man "out of the Whirlwind" and thunders a reply:

> Where wast thou when I laid the foundations
>   of the Earth?
> Declare if thou hast the understanding.
> Who determined the measures thereof,
>   if thou knowest?
> Or who stretched the line upon it?
> . . . When the morning stars sang together,
> And all the sons of God shouted for joy?

Tell me if you can, rational animal, philosopher, scientist.

Or who shut up the sea with doors,
When it broke forth, and issued
  out of the womb . . . ?
And said: "Thus far shalt thou come,
  but no further;
And here shall thy proud waves be stayed"?

Hast thou commanded the morning
  since thy days began,
and caused the dayspring to know its place?
Hast thou entered into the springs of the sea?
Or hast thou walked in the recesses of the deep?
Have the gates of death been revealed unto thee?
Or hast thou seen the gates of the shadow of death?
Hast thou surveyed unto the breadth of the Earth?
Declare, if thou knowest it all.

In other, profane, words: I made this world, not you, and
it is for you to live in it, meaning or no meaning, whether
it appears to your frail mind and daunted spirit just or un-
just, secure or precarious, good or evil, worthy or not of
your travail. For you are but a man, and know nothing.
Now speak, if you dare! Job declares only that he is

  . . . of small account;
  What shall I answer thee?
  I lay my hand upon my mouth.

But God is implacable, and continues to challenge man:

Canst thou draw out leviathan with a fish-hook?

Or press down his tongue with a cord?
Or bore his jaw through with a hook?
Will he make supplications unto thee? . . .
Will he make a covenant with thee . . . ?

Who then is able to stand before Me?
Who hath given Me anything before hand, that I
    should repay him?
Whatsoever is under the whole heaven is mine.

At the time of Hobbes, man had not yet been with God
when He created a world out of the void; had not yet entered into the recesses of the deep and walked therein; had
not yet surveyed the breadth of the Earth; or split the atom
of God. The whole fantastic adventure of modern science
had scarcely begun. It is, then, an astonishingly proud
Hobbes who accepts God's challenge to do combat, one
creator against the other.

Job at the last capitulates. I have, he says, uttered

. . . that which I understood not,
Things too wonderful for me, which I knew not . . . .
Wherefore I abhor my words, and repent,
Seeing I am dust and ashes.

But Hobbes will not abhor his words, will not repent. Dust
and ashes? Hobbes casts defiance at God—and at His han-
diwork, Nature. In the Book of Job, leviathan is depicted
as a monster of terrifying powers and dimensions: "his
sneezings flash forth light"; "out of his mouth go burning
torches"; "out of his nostrils goeth smoke"; "in his neck

abideth strength"; "the flakes of his flesh cannot be moved"; "his heart is as firm as stone." Nature, unyielding and inscrutable, utterly daunts Job; its horror challenges Hobbes, on the other hand, to devise a scheme.

He says in effect, that's not bad, not bad at all, for a beginner. But wait till You see what we men can do. Hobbes the man takes on God and God's Nature. What is more, he takes them on by his intelligence alone. Hobbes fashions his own fierce monster, his own *Leviathan*, an artificial creature to rival God's natural monster. Then Hobbes the man confronts God in the whirlwind and demands:

> Will he make supplications to *Thee*?
> Will he make a covenant with *Thee*?
> Who then is able to stand before me?
> Who hath given *me* anything beforehand, that I
>   should repay him?

> Whatsoever is under the whole heaven is *mine*.

Whatsoever is within the whole commonwealth belongs to Hobbes the man. And Hobbes is as proud as God.

We know what a fearful man Thomas Hobbes was; that when he was born his mother, in Hobbes' chilling words, "had brought forth twins—myself and fear." We know that he feared to lie abed in his room at night, alone, lest thieves attack him for the wealth they imagined he might possess. We know that Hobbes played tennis well into old age, not because he particularly enjoyed the game, but because he hoped it might prolong life a little; that he sang every evening at the top of his lungs, not because he especially liked to sing, still less because he fancied he was blessed with a pleasant voice, but because he thought singing might add a year or two. We know that Hobbes drank spirits at specified intervals, but not because he was by nature dissolute. He was not. Instead, he would gulp a few draughts, leave the room, cast the evil from his system, then return to the conversation having missed scarcely a word. This he did not for pleasure but for the sake of his health; not for enjoyment but to appease the passions setting up a continuous howl within; not from willfulness but, according to his own testimony, from fear.

Hobbes regarded his life, and that of every man who had the misfortune to resemble him temperamentally, as "an estate like to that of *Prometheus*. For as *Prometheus* (which interpreted is, *The Prudent Man*) was bound to the hill *Caucasus*, a place of large prospect, where, an Eagle feeding on his liver, devoured in the day, as much as was repayred in the night: So that man, which looks too far before him, in the care of future time, hath his heart all the day long, gnawed on by feare of death, poverty, or other calamity; and has no repose nor pause of his anxiety, but in sleep." Actually, Hobbes meant the eternal sleep, death. He was a master psychologist who knew only too well the anatomy of anxiety. Hobbes was one of the first of the moderns to explore the significance of dreams, fantasies, and hallucinations. And he knew that sleep provides no certain respite. True repose comes only with annihilation.

We also know that in politics Hobbes was haunted by the fear of disorder, anarchy, and civil war; that his solution was unqualified submission to a sovereign power and the resignation of all individual claims, save the ultimate one to self-preservation. His very name conveys as much to all interested in politics and political thought. Yet Hobbes was a most complex thinker, perhaps the most powerful political philosopher since Aristotle. He, of all thinkers, has deserved better of his critics.

It is my thesis that Hobbes' celebrated "state of nature" is not an historical account, although it contains certain historical overtones. Nor do I believe that it is meant to serve, as he himself appears on occasion to suggest, primarily as an analytic device. That Hobbes carries "man out of a state of nature into civil society" has long been a commonplace. Yet I am persuaded that the state of nature Hobbes divined is instead perpetual, a metaphorical description of what moves us all as creatures. The manifestations of the state of perpetual nature within are ordinary fancies, dreams, and idle thoughts. Its outward expression is found in conflict and competition between individuals, in what, according to Hobbes, we euphemistically call society. And it takes its most highly mobilized and destructive form in political strife, which produces anxiety and leads to physical pain and death. Because the unstructured political condition was, for Hobbes, one of unrelieved terror, he set out to provide the missing structure, fully aware of the difficulties involved in such an attempt owing to the persistence of the anti-social passions.

In the face of these difficulties Hobbes could not possibly hope to succeed by imposing his solution upon the public sphere alone. Since it is impossible to root out entirely what is perpetual and natural in human beings, namely, their hedonistic and destructive impulses, these must be either suppressed or stilled. The destructive passions are to be suppressed, kept from erupting into actual behavior by the organization of political life around the one central passion, that of self-preservation. This passion may be touched most effectively by a fear of retaliation, what men call punishment. Thus political life is organized around the reality of power. This feature of Hobbes' thought has provided the chief text for most commentaries by political writers. Hobbes is the theorist of political terror, mitigated by the submission to legitimate power.

But there is another feature of his thought that has scarcely received attention at all: Hobbes' scheme not only for suppressing the outward expression of anti-social passions, but for stilling them within. Hobbes proposes to accomplish this prodigy as well. He means to have invention, the expression of reason, triumph over spontaneity, the expression of passion. He places his ultimate trust in that greatest and most fundamental of all human inventions, language, which is the parent to reason. He means to strike the destructive passions dumb by depriving them of a suitable vocabulary. Words are his soldiers, sentences his regiments, books his armies. If a vocabulary of ethics, law, and politics entirely neutral in tone may be insinuated into men's thoughts and imposed upon their speech, it might serve to anesthetize the murderous passions within us all.

If we could but know "the nature of human actions" as distinctly as we know "the nature of quantity in geometrical figures, the strength of avarice and ambition . . . would presently faint and languish; and mankind should enjoy . . . immortal peace." To induce the passions to faint and languish, to achieve immortal peace: how worthy is Hobbes' effort to meet the challenge of God, since to Hobbes the passions belong to God and to God's creation, but the reason and its inventions belong only to men. In Hobbes' words we have some intimation of his hopes beyond the sphere of politics narrowly construed. The commentators have been so hypnotized by Hobbes' new *Leviathan* as a creation to overawe men that they have virtually ignored Hobbes as creator, Hobbes himself out of the whirlwind.

Hobbes first heightens our terror by conjuring up our deepest and hitherto nameless dread, and compels us to dwell with it for awhile. We are horrified, at the same time transfixed, and read on. When we are drawn almost to the breaking point, Hobbes names men's dread and we discover, to our immense relief, that it was not a wholly personal dread after all, but one shared by our fellows and stemming largely from political circumstance. Which means that we are far from incurable: our dread may be laid to rest by treatment that is *rational* and *public* in character. As Prometheus, Hobbes offers us the gift of solace, bidding us warm ourselves at his fire and cheering the darkness of our fears. And as creator, Hobbes would wish us never to forget that it is Prometheus's fire that warms and comforts us, the fire of Prometheus and no other. Prometheus might indeed be The Prudent Man, tortured on Caucasus by endless anxieties; he is also The Prideful Man who snatches fire from the gods to light men's way.

Now when we reflect upon this spectacle there seems something vaguely familiar about it, this being carried to the brink of annihilation where we are almost torn to pieces, only to be restored to a blessed wholeness at the end. The art of Hobbes is the art of the poet, never mind that his aim is to impose the spirit of science upon political thought and practice. We have witnessed it before, that foreboding, that whirring of demons: is it not the very rhythm of *Hamlet* and of *Macbeth* and of *Othello*? All begin by unleashing the terrifying powers of darkness; all end by reestablishing legitimate order. And at every step of the way our own fears, and hopes, are enlisted by the playwright the better to prepare us for the final resolution.

What I am suggesting is that a reading of *Leviathan* itself is meant to induce, *within our own being*, the psychological experience of political dread, then the glimmer of hope promised by the Idea—the Promethean gift of the theorist—and finally, the clear sunlit day of political tranquillity. To concentrate exclusively upon the explicit *content* of the theory is to slight the *craft*, as well as the dramatic imagination of the political theorist. We still read *Leviathan* after three centuries not because many of us have ever experienced the actual trauma of political dissolution—although the world sometimes seems to be drawing perilously close to that—but because we have all experienced the threat to the self implicit in the dread of personal dissolution. Like all great political theorists, Hobbes conjures up by an act of imagination, then deploys by an act of poetry, what trembles just beneath the consciousness of us all.

I

The appeal of the classical philosopher had been to the pride of the exceptional man. The appeal of Hobbes is to the fear of the ordinary man. Plato's ultimate, though perhaps forlorn, hope had been the appearance in the world of the philosopher-king. The writings of Cicero and Seneca were addressed not to subjects but to rulers. Even Machiavelli's target, at least in *The Prince*, was the prideful man of action rather than the common man. Hobbes appeals to the uneasiness of the English middle-class man, thereby inaugurating the age of ideology, in which political theorists, like politicians, seek to influence directly the conduct of the citizens. Pride or the desire for honor is too slippery a foundation upon which to build a politics of tranquillity in the restless modern world.

Hobbes seeks to erect his system not upon the gains to which men may aspire, but to their fear of what they stand to lose by refusing obedience. He tries to persuade men to offer up their spontaneous natures in order to guarantee their preservation. Frequently as men and women grow old and their grasp on life becomes fiercer because more precarious, they are required to sacrifice a limb or an internal organ to their continued preservation. None do so willingly, but only because they must if they would survive. Yet Hobbes requests a part of each of us in our prime. Like an insurance salesman, he tries to convince us to pay up now in order to go in peace.

To brood on the annihilation of life leads inevitably to despair. Hobbes proposes not only to arrange a bargain for us with a Sovereign—we resign our infernal private conscience and he will protect us—but also to brood for us upon the vicissitudes of existence that we ourselves might avoid anxiety. At a price, however. His price is that we mutually agree henceforth to discuss the human condition in his terms, rather than ours; that we discuss it in terms of reason and science, rather than of the passions—what Hobbes calls superstition, myth, and theology. To the Sov-

ereign we yield up our judgment. To the Scientist we surrender our understanding. We are paying for that fateful
bargain to this very day.

Anxiety, despair, and dread of annihilation are the most
prominent features of Hobbes' state of nature. And since
these are always with us, his state of nature cannot be
merely historical or analytic. It resides within us and is
perpetual. For it belongs to the realm of Nature, which is
God's, rather than to the realm of Invention, which is
Man's. The external expression of man's passionate nature
is to be found in society. In an earlier work, *De Cive*,
Hobbes invites us to observe what men do when they meet
in society:

> if they meet for traffic, it is plain every man regards
> not his fellow, but his business; if to discharge some
> office, a certain market-friendship is begotten, which
> hath more of jealousy in it than true love, and
> whence factions sometimes may arise, but good will
> never; if for pleasure, and recreation of mind, every
> man is wont to please himself most with those
> things which stir up laughter [by means of which he
> may ridicule the other man] . . . by comparison of
> [the] other man's infirmities. . . . But for the most
> part, in these kinds of meetings, we wound the ab-
> sent; their whole life, sayings, actions are examined,
> judged, condemned; nay, it is very rare, but some
> present receive a fling before they part, so as his
> reason was not ill, who was wont always at parting
> to go out last. And these are indeed the true de-
> lights of society, unto which we are carried by na-
> ture, that is, by those passions which are incident
> to all creatures. . . .

Such, such are the joys. And we are led to those joys not by Invention but by "nature, that is, by those passions which are incident to all creatures." "All society therefore is either for gain, or for glory; that is, not so much for love of our fellows, as for the love of ourselves." And the origin of society is to be sought not in the good will men might feel toward one another but in their mutual fear and distrust.

Thus we see how Nature, common to men as well as to all other creatures, is expressed in society. In its most destructive form, however, it makes its appearance in politics. "If now to this natural proclivity of men, to hurt each other, which they derive from their passions . . . you add . . . perpetual jealousies and suspicions on all hands," over the claims and evasions of rights—namely, passionate politics—the natural estate of men is war. "For what is war, but that same time in which the will of contesting by force is fully declared, either by words or deeds? The time remaining [that is, the rest of the time when we only *desire* to tear our fellows limb from limb], is termed peace."

What then is to be the resolution, how might peace be achieved? In *Leviathan* Hobbes offers a twofold solution, each aspect political in character. One is expressly legal, the other psychological or, more properly, pedagogical. In one side of the solution—the legal—the nature of man is suppressed. He dare not act for fear of retribution by a sovereign power which stands above the laws and which is their creator. Public life is to be organized about the fear of death. Conversely, the will to self-preservation sustains obedience. In the other side—the pedagogical—the passions are not suppressed, they are quieted. *And that is the work for the intellectual, for the man of words rather than of action, for the scientist and not the king.* To understand the true Legislator in Hobbes, his whole politics, one must combine the offices of Sovereign and Scientist.

Remarkably, although Englishmen and Americans in particular have paid much attention to Hobbes' legal theory, they have rarely experienced a Hobbesian legal system pure and simple. But the genius of Hobbes was to insinuate the materials of his pedagogy into the minds of those who followed. In the Anglo-American constitutional tradition Hobbes, as he fervently hoped he would, was the last powerful political thinker to treat openly, and in plain words, of such sublime topics as fear, anxiety, envy, hatred, love, vainglory, appetite, sensuality, repentance, anger, laughter, shame, indignation, and death.

Hobbes looked upon the many faces of passion, and learned their names. Then, as if doing magic, he transformed them in his magnificent logic machine. Into the machine went the likes of envy and fear and anxiety and pain and murder, out came sovereignty and positive law; out came proposition, cause and effect, identity and difference, out came motions and magnitudes, sense and behavior, liberty and necessity. It was Hobbes' political theory above all that provided passage between the virile— and dangerous—thought of the Italian Renaissance and the tight-lipped style of modern Liberalism.

Not only Madison's Constitution, but the political theory of Franklin and Paine, even of John C. Calhoun, reflects the influence of the vocabulary of Thomas Hobbes. More than that, it reflects his mood. Not the mood of the passions going in, but the science coming out the other end. Since Hobbes, we discuss politics and law in terms not of art but of mechanics; not of envy but of interest; not of retribution but of balance; not in terms of unremitting war but of contract. Hobbes, then, is not merely Legislator but Censor, not only Legal Theorist but Teacher. No wonder the political rhetoric of the past decade confounds us. It marks a leap backward in time to a pre-Hobbesian politics. Still, Hobbes' political words remain the words of Legitimacy.*

---

*Benjamin Franklin: "As the *Desire* of being freed from Uneasiness is equal to the *Uneasiness*, and the *Pleasure* of satisfying the Desire equal to the *Desire*, the *Pleasure* thereby produc'd must necessarily be equal to the *Uneasiness* or *Pain* which produces it: Of three lines, A, B, and C, if A is equal to B, and B to C, C must be equal to A. And as our *Uneasinesses* are always remov'd by some Means or other, it follows that *Pleasure* and *Pain* are in their Nature inseparable: So many Degrees as one Scale of the Balance descends, so many exactly the other ascends; and one cannot rise or fall without the Fall or Rise of the other: 'Tis impossible to taste of *Pleasure*, without feeling its preceding proportionate *Pain*; or to be sensible of *Pain*, without having its necessary Consequent *Pleasure*: The *highest Pleasure* is only Consciousness of Freedom from the *deepest Pain*, and Pain is not Pain to us unless we ourselves are sensible of it. They go Hand in Hand; they cannot be divided." (*A Dissertation on Liberty and Necessity, Pleasure and Pain.*)

Thomas Paine: "for as the greater weight will always carry up the less, and as the wheels of a machine are put in motion by one, it only remains to know which power in the constitution has the most weight, for that will govern; and though the others, or a part of them, may clog, or, as the phrase is, check the rapidity of the motion, yet so long as they cannot stop it, their endeavours will be ineffectual: The first moving power will at last have its way, and what it wants in speed is supplied by time." (*Common Sense.*)

Calhoun: "In order to have a clear and just conception of the nature and object of government, it is indispensable to understand correctly what that constitution or law of our nature is, in which government originates; or, to express it more fully and accurately—that law, without which government would not, and with which, it must necessarily exist. Without this, it is as impossible to lay any solid foundation for the science of government, as it would be to lay one for that of astronomy, without a like understanding of that constitution or law of the material world, according to which the several bodies composing the solar system mutually act on each other, and by which they are kept in their respective spheres." (*Disquisition on Government.*)

It would seem that whether contemplating the psychology of the individual or making a revolution or writing a constitution or defending a "peculiar institution," Americans have found the scientific vocabulary of Thomas Hobbes, reinforced by the specific theories of Isaac Newton, most convenient.

To return to the combination of Sovereign and Scientist in Hobbes' political theory, the need for it is prompted by the view that men are by nature incorrigibly egoistic. In a natural state, where there must always be a scarcity of goods by definition—the selfish ego is never satisfied—a condition of perpetual warfare exists among all men. How much wealth is enough? Ask any rich man.* Because there are no mutually acceptable rules, all is fair in the struggle for existence and powers. Two-legged beasts of prey forage everywhere without let or hindrance, save that introduced by sporadic coercion or fear. For every man has by nature a perfect right to every thing. And obviously, since his most precious possession is his own existence, the fundamental law of nature is self-preservation. All the laws of nature might exist internally, in conscience perhaps. But in the absence of security, none may be enforced. To achieve security, commonwealths are established among men.

Commonwealth arises not from Nature but from reason. It is an artificial product, an Invention of the prudent reason out of fear and the experience, over countless generations, of solitude and pain and violent death. Commonwealth is the creation, by agreement, of sovereign power to which the subject owes all due obedience, so long as the Sovereign has the power and the will to protect him. The Sovereign is not a party to the original contract, hence is

---

*J. Paul Getty, in an interview published in the San Francisco *Chronicle*, February 7, 1974: "I've always had a place for every dollar that came in. I've never seen the day where I could say that I felt rich. Generally, you worry about paying the bills." That Getty would have felt at home in Hobbes' world is attested by the obvious fact that he carried that world about inside himself.

not limited by the laws, but is their creator and stands above them. The Sovereign enjoys full powers of peace and war, of judicature, legislation, and censorship. The subject enjoys full liberty to obey. But his one inviolable right is that of preservation, for the guarantee of which he entered into civil society in the first place. As for the rest, the liberty of the subject is to be discovered in the silence of the laws.

When not in the debt of the Sovereign, the subject may, however, refuse recognition to him for sufficient reason; for instance, if he is captured and forced to acknowledge a new Sovereign on pain of death; or if the Sovereign resigns in effect, or abdicates formally; or in the event the Sovereign is taken or put to flight by another more powerful Sovereign.

The authority of the Sovereign over the citizens is not divisible or alienable, nor is the public obligation of the citizens. They may not resign any part of it to leagues, cabals, or factions. Law is the command of the Sovereign; and the task of interpreting the law is solely the province of the Sovereign.

If Hobbes' theories of sovereignty and obligation seem stern, it is crucial to recognize that in his view men and states are always poised between pride and fear. Pride is the ideal expression of the mood of vitality in the state of nature. Fear is the ideal expression of dread and of the longing for security. Pride leads backward into a state of war. Fear leads forward into a state of civil society. Thus the state of nature and civil society are in constant tension. Given this tension, the role of law and of political education is identical. It is to tip the balance to civil society by evoking the fear of violent death: the citizen's fear in the case of the Sovereign, and the reader's in the case of the political theorist. In such a view, there exists everywhere nothing less than perpetual political crisis.

This important consideration helps explain Hobbes' twofold appeal to law and science. It also helps account for the extravagance of Hobbes' descriptive vocabulary when he sets the problem, as compared to the austerity of his analytic vocabulary when he offers his solutions. We get an intimation, in words, of what the present political condition is; and we get an intimation, in words, of what *Leviathan* will be in fact. By his art Hobbes propels his contemporary audience out of their complacent view that seventeenth-century England is a civilized society and convinces them that they live in a jungle. Terror awaits them around the next corner, violent death stalks them down the next dark street. He is utterly devastating. Regardless of the veracity of his psychological science, Hobbes himself is a master psychologist. He is forever placing us in peril by means of his poetry, then rescuing us in the nick of time by his science.

Although on occasion "man to man is a kind of god," it is nonetheless true that at least as often "man to man is an arrant wolf." It doesn't take much reading in Hobbes to develop a picture of his natural man, to see why Hobbes himself is so terrified of this creature. His celebrated catalogue of the passions in *Body, Man, and Citizen* is a good example. It is an example as well of Hobbes' adroitness in manipulating our fears. "The comparison of the life of man to a race," he writes, "though it hold not in every part, yet it holdeth so well for this purpose, that we may thereby both see and remember almost all the passions. . . . But this *race* we must suppose to have no other *goal*, nor other *garland*, but being foremost; and in it:

To endeavor, is *appetite.*
To be remiss, is *sensuality.* [Imagine!]
To consider them behind, is *glory.*
To consider them before, is *humility.*
To lose ground with looking back, *vain glory.*
To be holden, *hatred.*
To turn back, *repentance.*
To be in breath, *hope.*
To be weary, *despair.*
To endeavor to overtake the next, *emulation.*
To supplant or overthrow, *envy.*
To resolve to break through a stop, foreseen,
    courage.
To break through a sudden stop, *anger.*
To break through with ease, *magnanimity.*
To lose ground by little hindrances, *pusillanimity.*
To fall on the sudden, is disposition to *weep.*
To see another fall, is disposition to *laugh.*
To see one out-gone whom we would not, is *pity.*
To see one out-go whom we would not, is
    indignation.
To hold fast by another, is to *love.*
To carry him on that so holdeth, is *charity.*
To hurt one's-self for haste, is *shame.*
Continually to be out-gone, is *misery.*
Continually to out-go the next before, is *felicity.*
And to forsake the course, is to *die.*

To forsake the course is to die: what clearer evidence

that the state of nature is perpetual and that society, if not carefully hedged by rules, tends merely to reflect that perpetual inner turmoil of man? In this rough-and-tumble, where everybody is out to best everybody else, we spy an occasional foot thrust out to trip the unsuspecting runner, an occasional elbow in the ribs, a furtive nudge over the side. Transported into public life this competition breeds a society of rivalry, fraud, and remorselessness where, according to *Leviathan,* "men have no pleasure (but on the contrary a great deale of griefe) in keeping company, where there is no power able to overawe them all." The only recourse is a well-lighted track, a set of firm rules, and a disinterested judge.

Man is stubbornly quarrelsome, and the causes are to be found in his natural proclivity to competition, suspicion, and lust for glory. Competition induces men to invade others for gain, diffidence to invade for personal safety, and glory to invade for reputation. "The first use Violence, to make themselves Masters of other men's persons, wives, children, and cattell; the second, to defend them; the third, for trifles, as a word, a smile, a different opinion, and any other signe of undervalue." Without a common power to overawe them all "every man is Enemy to every other man; . . . there is no place for Industry; because the fruit thereof is uncertain: and consequently no Culture of the Earth, no Navigation, . . . no commodious Building; no Instruments of moving, and removing such things as require much force; no Knowledge of the face of the Earth; no account of Time; no Arts; no Letters; no Society; and which is worst of all, continuall feare, and danger of violent death; And the life of man, solitary, poore, nasty, brutish, and short."

"It may seem strange to some man, that has not well weighed these things," Hobbes writes, "that Nature should thus dissociate, and render men apt to invade, and destroy one another." Yet should rational inference prove insufficient, let any man examine his own actions day in, day out. Let him "consider with himselfe, when taking a journey, he armes himselfe, and seeks to go well accompanied; when going to sleep, he locks his dores; when even in his house he locks his chests; and this when he knowes there bee Lawes, and publike Officers, armed, to revenge all injuries shall bee done him; what opinion he has of his fellow subjects, when he rides armed; of his fellow Citizens, when he locks his dores; and of his children, and servants, when he locks his chests. Does he not there as much accuse mankind by his actions, as I do by my words?"

The picture of man which Hobbes creates, and the dread he arouses in us convinces us that the state of nature is always with us, threatening to burst out and engulf us. Wherever the passions overwhelm men, life indeed must be solitary, brutish, and painfully short. Hobbes persuades us that one way to subdue the passions before they lead us to mutual destruction is by accepting a common power to overawe us all.*

---

*Hobbes' state of nature is as old as the Old Testament, his task that of a modern Moses—which touches upon the reasons for my not having included John Locke in this study. First is the fact that in his work political imagination of the order displayed by Machiavelli, Hobbes, and Rousseau is conspicuously absent. Second, Hobbes, desperate Old Testament thinker that he is, creates the political universe; Locke smooths some of the rough edges and induces us to forget the mounds of bodies upon which the modern state rests. Where in Hobbes the fearful prospect of an outright reversion to barbarism is clearly before us, Locke frequently exudes a sweet reasonableness whose consequence, whether or not intended, is to lull us into the false belief that a settlement, thank God, has already been concluded.

Where does this common power originate? Hobbes locates its origins in confrontation: men emerge at last from
their dark caves to face one another in dread. Should they
fight, out of the battle there arises a common power established by the conqueror; should they perchance agree, out
of their agreement arises a common power. It is agreement
founded in mutual fear of imminent death, rather than conquest based upon pride, that preoccupies Hobbes. "And
Reason suggesteth convenient Articles of Peace, upon which
men may be drawn to agreement."

Even after the agreement has been concluded and
Commonwealth brought into existence, Hobbes relies upon
fear to sustain it. There are but two imaginable passions in
men upon which we might rely for stability. "And these
are either a Feare of the consequences of breaking their
word; or a Glory, or Pride in appearing not to need to
breake it. This later is a Generosity too rarely found to be
presumed on, especially in the pursuers of Wealth, Command, or sensuall Pleasure; which are the greatest part of
Mankind. The Passion to be reckoned upon, is Fear."

First there must be present a fear sufficient to have
men contract together, then a fear sufficient to induce
them to keep their word. This latter fear is supplied by the
Sovereign, the something "else required (besides Covenant) to make their Agreement constant and lasting; which
is a Common Power, to keep them in awe, and to direct
their actions to the Common Benefit." They confer "all
their power and strength upon one Man, or upon one Assembly of men, that they may reduce all their Wills . . .
unto one Will: which is as much to say, to appoint one
Man, or Assembly of men, to beare their Person; and every
one to owne, and acknowledge himselfe to be Author of [all

acts], in those things which concerne the Common Peace and Safetie; and therein to submit their Wills, every one to his Will, and their Judgements, to his Judgement. . . . This done, the Multitude so united in one Person, is called a COMMON-WEALTH. . . . This is the Generation of that great LEVIATHAN, or rather (to speake more reverently) of that *Mortall God*, to which wee owe under the *Immortall God*, our peace and defence." And who, pray, was more reverent than Thomas Hobbes?

The final step is to forge "Artificial Chains, called *Civill Lawes*, which they themselves, by mutuall covenants, have fastened at one end to the lips of. . . the Soveraigne. . .and at the other end to their own Ears." Thus are the private and public realms drawn together: thus is the conscience of man overwhelmed by command, drowned out by the authoritative voice of the managers.*

Still, despite everything, as Hobbes well knew, men are irascible. To their irascibility, as well as their ambition and stupidity, Hobbes attributes the death of Leviathan. In his consideration of the demise of the monster we become more aware of its creator's dualistic theory of rule, as we perceive a shift from political power to political science, from the word *power* to the power of *words*.

II

"God said to Adam, that on the day he should eat of

---

*Rousseau was in the next century to invent a "Camera-Sovereign," who kept us in his sights at all times. In this figure, Hobbes' creation was a "Telephone-Sovereign," on a one-way hookup.

the forbidden fruit, he should certainly die; from that time forward," Hobbes writes, "he was a dead man by sentence." Only the execution of the sentence remains. Remember Hobbes' keen sense of mortality and his desperate attempt to stay alive by sheer intelligence. *Leviathan* is meant to postpone the death sentence as long as possible for every man, but at a price: the sacrifice of private conscience to public judgment, handed down by the Sovereign; and the sacrifice of personal understanding to scientific, that is, public, knowledge.

But states also exist under sentence of death. Besides prescribing for the longevity of the citizens, Hobbes advises on the health and sickness of the state itself. What most often kills Leviathan is precisely the failure of the citizens to keep their end of the bargain by paying up for protection received. They insist instead upon viewing private conscience as the ultimate source of public judgment. True, there are other causes for the death of the state— attempts, for instance, to subject the Sovereign to the laws. Or the insistence upon an absolute right to private property. There are also ill-advised schemes for dividing or diffusing Sovereign power. But these, according to Hobbes, are but "scabs" and "biles" upon Leviathan.

The willful substitution of private conscience for public command, however, remains *the* mortal disease. It is an unfailing killer. It kills by hydrophobia or epilepsy, that is, Rebellion; and by poison, that is, Sedition, its venom being the dogmas that generate passion rather than abetting science (religious superstition, pre-Christian poetry, mythical history—called by men "tradition") and the "Philosophy of the Greeks, especially Aristotle."

Hobbes' picture of the Greek schools is stunning. We see loafers and no-goods lolling about, talking, talking, talking. Listening breathlessly are a bevy of pretty youths, unaware of the hidden motives of the old lechers who are their teachers. The whole proud Platonic system Hobbes regards as but "an honorable pretense for the old to haunt the company of the young and beautiful." The manners of youth are thus corrupted. Hobbes would rather their morals had been corrupted instead, but a single generation debauched, for the passions, once deflected to philosophy, had produced a body of ideas that has dominated the entire world with its falsehoods, debauching us all.

Parenthetically, these and other assorted passages from Hobbes' work show up a certain flaw in his temperament as a thinker. What I have in mind is this. Suppose Hobbes was serious in the motivation he imputes to Socrates and Plato and Aristotle—that their ingenuity was bent to seducing youth, and that their political philosophies were largely instrumental to that purpose—he might well have asked what fantastic quality in human nature, or in human culture, is responsible for transmuting a quite ordinary sensual lust into a majestic philosophical system, whose consequences far transcend its (clandestine) purposes. His failure to press this line of inquiry indicates the absence in Hobbes of a playful spirit, at least when it came to discussing the Greeks. Had such a spirit not been wanting, perhaps we would not have had to wait so long—until Nietzsche and Dostoyevsky and Freud—to glimpse the remarkable deflective powers of humanity; to appreciate art and philosophy and science as also reflecting, but now only indirectly, certain animal drives in us all. Nor does

Hobbes seek to turn his criticisms to his own argument concerning the dangerous passions lurking even within the breasts of our hallowed philosophical forebears. Instead, he felt constrained to vent his wrath. Whenever he spoke of the Greeks, Hobbes seemed to lose his composure as a worldly philosopher, his words becoming more malicious and vengeful than detached or even sardonic.

To return to Hobbes' indictment of the Greeks, they loved, he says, to "prate" and "loyter," and from such sloth and indulgence—traits anathema to any sober, responsible middle-class Englishman—there arose the imprisoning metaphysical claptrap from which the world has yet to extricate itself. Hobbes viewed the natural philosophy of the schools as "rather a Dream than Science, and set forth in senseless and insignificant Language." The moral philosophy of the Greeks was worse yet, "but a description of their own Passions." The Greeks insisted upon making "The Rules of *Good*, and *Bad*, by their own *Liking*, and *Disliking*: By which means, in so great diversity of taste, there is nothing generally agreed on; but every one doth (as far as he dares) whatsoever seemeth good in his owne eyes, to the subversion of Common-Wealth."

Nothing for Hobbes, not even sloth, could equal for sheer destructiveness the doctrine that each is to be the judge of what the Commonwealth requires. Not that these Greeks are notable for their crude hedonism, or for their adherence to any dogma remotely resembling the unalienable rights of conscience. For Hobbes they were dangerous enough in their intellectual pride. Thus he states "that scarce any thing can be more absurdly said in naturall Philosophy, than that which now is called *Aristotles Metaphy-*

siques; nor more repugnant to Government, than much of
that hee hath said in his *Politiques;* nor more ignorantly,
than a great part of his *Ethiques.*"

These pernicious doctrines, mingled with a witless but
pious Christianity, had captured the English schools and
long held their scholars enthralled. There, they prepared
the ground for Sedition by affording ready support for the
notion that private judgments of good and evil—that is, the
dictates of so-called Christian conscience—are morally superior to the commands of public authority. Men had become so habituated to the attitudes of Aristotle who, Hobbes
suggests, was a fraud—a coward who feared the fate of
Socrates—that they were led away from "obeying the Laws
of their Countrey." The schoolmen had terrorized the better half of the community with false doctrines and base su-
perstitions, "with empty names; as men fright Birds from
the Corn with an empty doublet, a hat, and a crooked
stick." The empty doublet is Aristotle, the hat Independen-
dency, the crooked stick the nameless fears provoked by
a primitive Christianity.

Another heinous crime perpetrated by Greek philosophy, a crime related to the elevation of individual conscience, was to delude men into castigating "all manner of
Common-Wealths but the Popular (such as was at that time
the state of Athens)." It had become the custom in England
to regard even kingship as tyranny, a legacy of Greek political thought. "All Kings they [the Greeks] called Tyrants." Abjuring all tyrants, they had argued that "not Men
should govern, but the Laws. What man, that has his naturall Senses, though he can neither write nor reade, does
not find himself governed by them he fears, and believes

can kill or hurt him when he obeyeth not?" In Hobbes' total system of governance by hook and by book, neither law nor the sword is to be spared.

The disease under investigation is Sedition, and the remedy seems clear enough: root out these several influences upon the individual and collective passions. The Sovereign has the authority to forbid their teaching. But, not possessing the sword, Hobbes himself must use words, both by publishing *Leviathan* and by the specific counsel he offers to combat the Greek contamination. Once translate the "strange and barbarous" words of the Ancients—their "Jargon"—into the vernacular of English or French, and their magic spell will have been broken. One result of the magic of the Ancients was "not only to hide Truth, but also to make men think they [already] have it, and desist from further search." Amen. Unfortunately, Hobbes was to propose nothing less destructive of the search he so much wished to stimulate. For Hobbes, truth is to be sought in one way, and in one way only: through systematic investigation of the passions and possibilities of man. But truth is also to be expressed in one way, and in one way only, in the austere language of mathematical reason.

Let us turn now to the role played by Rebellion in the death of the state. For Rebellion to occur, three factors must be present in any situation: discontent, pretense of right, and hope of success. For it "were madness to attempt without hope, when to fail, is to die the death of a traitor." (Hobbes was so thoroughly utilitarian in outlook that he could not begin to conceive the motivations of martyrs, nihilists, or even romantics. He dismisses them as subject simply to "madnesse.") When the three conditions—discontent, pretense of right, and hope of success—coincide, nothing is wanting "but a man of credit to set up the standard, and to blow the trumpet."

Foremost among the "pretenses to Rebellion" is the complaint that a particular "command is against . . . conscience." If such can be established by a man of persuasion, regardless how silly his ideas, the Rebellion stands a chance of success. For "Two things [are] necessary to an author of rebellion, much eloquence, and little wisdom." (If so, how like a rebel a schoolmaster is!) Again, even when treating of Rebellion, Hobbes stresses words and knowledge rather than organization and tactics. The leader of a Rebellion has to be a man of little wisdom; were he not, he would calculate the overwhelming odds against him and prefer despair to the meaningless death which awaits him. He has also to be a man of much eloquence, since Rebellion depends upon his capacity to arouse and direct the passions of the multitude. Scientific discourse tends to be "unpleasant to the hearer," owing to the attention it demands of him. But the rebel leader is prohibited from resorting to the language of science for still another reason. His vocation consists in turning good into bad and bad into good. He must be a gifted liar, an inciter of envy, hatred, and indignation, with a talent for "putting together passionate words, and applying them to the present passions of the hearer."

Hobbes concludes his discussion of Rebellion, and of the central role of speech in fomenting it—eloquence addressed to the latent passions of the audience—with the charming tale of the archetypical rebel, Medea, who employed her words as so many razor slashes to gain her diabolical ends. "The daughters of Pelias, king of Thessaly, desiring to restore their old decrepit father to the vigor of his youth, by the counsel of Medea, chopped him in pieces, and set him aboiling with I know not what herbs in a cauldron, but could not revive him again. So when eloquence and want of judgment go together, want of judgment, like the daughters of Pelias, consenteth, through eloquence, which is as the witchcraft of Medea, to cut the commonwealth in pieces, upon pretense or hope of reformation." The terror which political disorder held for Hobbes is plain: the alternative to absolute sovereignty is cannibalism.

What is there left to say? The body of Pelias (England) was being hacked to pieces before Hobbes' eyes by political, philosophical, moral, and theological eloquence, which is as the witchcraft of the politician, the philosopher, the moralist, and the ecclesiast. His daughters, the subjects, were but an audience duped into committing atrocities upon the father-state.

Ultimately Hobbes intends to fight fire with fire, to counteract words with other words, to reach down even to our anti-social passions and to quiet them by depriving them of a vocabulary in which they might be expressed; by his craft to strike them dumb.

The circle is closed: Hobbes first delivers *Leviathan*; he then establishes a regimen, nourishing and healthful, and goes on to diagnose the childhood diseases as well as the infirmities of old age; at the last he will request some kindly old Sovereign to activate *Leviathan* by turning political theory into political utility:

I am at the point of believing this my labour, as uselesse, as the Common-Wealth of *Plato*; For he also is of opinion that it is impossible for the disorders of State, and change of Governments by Civill Warre, ever to be taken away, till Soveraigns be Philosophers. But when I consider again, that the Science of Naturall Justice, is the only science necessary for Soveraigns, and their principall Ministers; and that they need not be charged with the Sciences Mathematicall, (as by *Plato* they are,) further, than by good Lawes to encourage men to the study of them; and that neither *Plato*, nor any other Philosopher hitherto, hath put into order, and sufficiently or probably proved all the Theoremes of Morall doctrine, that men may learn thereby, both how to govern, and how to obey; I recover some hope, that one time or other, this writing of mine, may fall into the hands of a Soveraigne, who will consider it himselfe, (for it is short, and I think clear,) without the help of any interesses, or envious Interpreter; and by the exercise of entire Soveraignty, in protecting the Publique teaching of it, convert this Truth of Speculation, into the Utility of Practice.

But Hobbes could not count upon gaining a hearing from any Sovereign actual or potential: hence his desperation to reach the citizens and subjects by himself, directly, through *Leviathan*. And his passion to persuade other thinkers, other teachers, of the truth of his utilitarianism and the utility of his truth.

Machiavelli had sought a Prince to bring the nation into being and to unify it; his emphasis was upon *action* and *acting*. Hobbes seeks a Sovereign to complete the task by legitimizing the artificial creature; his emphasis is upon *science* and *language*.

III

Norbert Wiener, the mathematician and founder of the science of cybernetics, once said that "Speech is a joint game by the talker and listener, against the forces of confusion." Speech is a game aimed at creating order. But there is a maxim drawn from Proverbs, found in the rules of deportment of the Benedictines of Monte Cassino, a silent order: "Mors et vita in manibus linguae." Life and death are controlled by the tongue. Speech can be a mortal weapon.

In Hobbes we encounter both perspectives. Writing in *Body, Man, and Citizen*, Hobbes contends that "*not the truth*, but the *image*, maketh passion: and a tragedy, well acted, affecteth no less than a murder." Hobbes wishes, as a teacher above all, to direct language against the forces of confusion. To do so he must impress upon us that speech has all too frequently been wielded as a mortal weapon in society.

The image makes passion, a tragedy affects no less than a murder. Hobbes saw it as the foremost task of the responsible intelligence to draw the curtain on tragedy and to substitute in its place scientific truth, so that, as in Plato, anti-social passions would cease to be made. The way to the passions is through words. The way from the passions to the external world is through actions. Talking itself is action. And, as we know, the most common activity in politics is talking. It follows that he who shapes men's words shapes their political passions.

I have used the word *passion* in practically every paragraph of my discussion. Even where I quote Hobbes to the effect that "man to man is an arrant wolf," however, and cite his use of words such as hatred or envy or fear, the discussion is still at a level of abstraction itself removed from passion—perhaps the effect Hobbes hoped to produce. Before seeking the link in Hobbes' thought between words and passions, I would like to portray the sense of the terrifying that the passions actually held for Hobbes.

When analyzing dominion, Hobbes considers the relations between fathers and sons. He concludes that if fathers did not have a tacit guarantee that their children would obey them, they would most likely abandon their offspring at birth. He "which giveth sustenance to another, whereby to strengthen him, hath received a promise of obedience in consideration thereof. For else it would be wisdom in men, rather to let their children perish, while they are infants, than to live in their danger or subjection, when they are grown." It is chilling to be told that between the members of the family and murder in cold blood stands only a truce between aggressor and victim. Less shocking to be sure since Freud, but shocking nevertheless. In the family the

> father, or he or she that bringeth up the child, have absolute power over him. Children therefore . . .

are in most absolute subjection to him . . . that preserveth them. And they may alienate them . . .by selling, or giving them, in adoption or servitude to others; or may pawn them for hostages, kill them for rebellion, or sacrifice them for peace, by the law of nature, when he or she, in his or her conscience, think it to be necessary.

If this be a law of nature, then there is no atrocity of which man in his natural state, that is, in the absence of coercion, is incapable. Hobbes had translated the *History* of Thucydides and had been duly impressed with the capacity of even the most civilized among us to lapse into a condition of frightful barbarism. If the state of nature could at last emerge from the darkness to which it had been consigned by Greek rationality and could overwhelm even Athens, then no men were to be spared the struggle to subdue their rebellious passions. That Hobbes actually thought in this way may be seen in the private behaviors he insists his Sovereign prohibit under severest penalty. Heading the list is "unnatural copulation." The Sovereign is to enact laws forbidding "such copulations as are against the use of nature"; "the promiscuous use of women"; and incest. The point is that Hobbes fully expects such conduct of men (even of English men) in the absence of formal laws. He places no trust whatever in private morality or traditional religion. For he is persuaded that "a private man living under the law of natural reason only" will do what his lusts impel him to do. The Sovereign must restrain him by positive law; Hobbes does so by cleansing the emotional environment of words that kindle lusts.

That our passions are unspeakably vile may be verified by simply permitting our everyday thoughts, our most ordinary fantasies, to rise to the level of the conscious. Whoever has deliberately done so must agree that filth and vileness are ever poised to invade the realm of consciousness. "The secret thought of a man run over all things, holy, profane, clean, obscene, grave, and light, without shame, or blame." Thus for a man, not a physician, "to write his extravagant, and pleasant fancies of the same, is as if a man, from being tumbled into the dirt, should come and present himselfe before good company." Each of us conceals within him a dirty little man raging for sensual license, bursting to express his vile thoughts in words, then to put those thoughts into action. These wild and extravagant passions would tear any society to pieces.

What else is intoxication but removing the inhibition to passion? The Romans had a saying: "In wine there is truth." Hobbes puts it this way: the "effect of wine, does but remove Dissimulation." The drunkard becomes his true, passionate self, his "natural" self—"Raging," "Loving," "Laughing"—all extravagantly, according to his "domineering Passions." Yet even the "most sober men, when they walk alone without care and employment of the mind, would be unwilling the vanity and Extravagance of their thoughts at that time should be publiquely seen: which is a confession, that Passions unguided, are for the most part meere Madnesse." All of us recapitulate, in our own lives, the universal experience of mankind. We tame ourselves, or are tamed; we move from "meere Madnesse" to structured, rational thought and conduct. But still the "Madnesse" lies dormant within us, to be liberated from time to time to commit its wild excesses in the world.

The state of nature is perpetual. It resides in men's passions, ever clamoring for release. Yet their uninhibited release would mean madness. Society would become a bacchanal, a frenzied dance around the Golden Calf. It is the task of the Sovereign to enforce, if not total abstinence, then at least a salutary temperance. It is the task of the Scientist so to employ the mind, in Hobbes' figure, that the individual will never walk alone, a victim to all sorts of crazy impulses crying out to him; but would be compelled to take along company, scientific preventives, words and charms, to help still the clamor. As for the social and political drunks, Hobbes will teach them to dread their pleasant intoxicating reveries.

IV

I should now like to attempt an overview of Hobbes' political theory as set down in *Leviathan*, to bring into relationship his legal with his linguistic ideas the better to appreciate his Legislation as a totality.

Man is by nature a beast of prey. Unlike the other creatures of the earth, he is essentially a solitary beast, by nature unfit for society, which most often merely provides an occasion for him to get what he wants, to invade and diminish others to his own advantage. The thoughts and fantasies of men recognize no limits. In our imaginations we pillage, we murder, we rape.

To admit this is not necessarily to condemn humanity. Because God made us this way, such thoughts and fantasies are quite natural. In the absence of convention even acting upon them is not to be condemned, for such action is natural as well. Each man by knowing himself also knows his fellows, and he cannot condemn in them the same impulses he discovers in himself. The human passions recognize no bounds, nor do they acknowledge a higher law, unaided.

Fortunately, there is one passion which disposes men to listen to the voice of reason. That passion is *fear*. Men fear pillage and death at the hands of others. When fear becomes powerful enough to overcome pride, which is the sense of omnipotence and immortality making us restless and obstinate and leading to war, men contract together to establish an artificial society, known as Commonwealth.

In the absence of a common power, however, Commonwealth alone guaranties nothing. There still needs to be created a power to overawe men by continued fear. That power is called Sovereignty. Through the laws the Sovereign establishes the criteria for social good and evil. What is "natural" in the absence of *Leviathan* becomes "unnatural" in the presence of *Leviathan*. The lips of the Sovereign are fastened to the ear of the subject as an externalized conscience. What men relinquish, then, is their frail, cunning, deceitful, self-destructive natural conscience. They agree mutually to suspend their pride. What they receive in return is protection. Instead of the natural conscience tempting us to flip the coin just one more time in the hope it will come up tails, the voice of the mortal God whispers in our ear: "Do it, and you're a dead man." Nature is dethroned. In her place sits the Sovereign, to his subjects as much an insurmountable calamity of nature as earthquake, flood, or famine.

Humankind thus departs the state of nature and presumably becomes "political," at least by Hobbes' criteria. But besides wishing to politicize the wolf, Hobbes entertains dreams of *civilizing* him. And since men of intellect do not have the sword at their disposal, they must use the only weapons they possess: words. Hobbes will civilize us by rooting out of our vocabulary all words with the potential to stimulate passionate action. This, it seems to me, is by far the greater challenge and the more daring enterprise. Hobbes will put a ring in the nose of the natural Leviathan. He will sterilize our very passions if he can.

"The effect of wine," Hobbes had said, "does but remove Dissimulation." Yet living together in peace seems to require nothing so much as concealing from one another, and even from ourselves, our raging, insatiable passions. Becoming civilized means learning pretenses. Freud once observed that mankind had taken a tremendous stride forward when men took to hurling invective at one another instead of spears. Hobbes would put an end even to such behavior, on the ground of its potential for activating violence. He was persuaded that culture, civil society, polite conversation, politics, are all artificial, sustained by a certain measure of dissimulation. That is why he could insist that it is a "law of nature, *That no man reproach, revile, deride, or any otherwise declare his hatred, contempt, or disesteem of any other.*" Once the passions begin to heat up, all the fierceness within boils to the surface. And the outcome is invariably mutual destruction. We simply cannot afford to tell each other the truth, at least as told us by the passions.

It is for this reason that Hobbes prefers monarchy

which, he says, is a "bulwark to the passions" because it requires no democratic assembly in which the passions of men may be "worked on"; where "the passions of these that are singularly moderate [become] altogether vehement; even as a great many coals, though but warm asunder, being put together, inflame one another." As for democracy, what is democracy but "an aristocracy of orators, interrupted sometimes with the temporary monarchy of one orator"?

Hobbes' task as political theorist, when he is addressing the subjects rather than the Sovereign, is to teach them political manners. He saw political theory essentially as education, and political education as Legislation. The Sovereign legislates through his laws. Hobbes legislates through his words.

Earlier political theorists, notably the Greeks, Hobbes regards as mere "pleaders" or "advocates" with the "faculty of *rhetoric* to seduce the jury." Hobbes alone assumes the stance of judge. He alone is the true educator, the unbiased political judge. A counselor of this kind is needed at the side of the King. The Sovereign would grant the Philosopher a share in his power. The Philosopher would grant the Sovereign a share in his science.

The laws may check passion, but only science has the techniques for uprooting it. Opinions formed over time are "made habitual" and, according to Hobbes, "cannot be taken away by force, and upon the sudden; they therefore must be taken away also by time and education." That is why Hobbes' solution must be twofold, both legal and pedagogical. His hope was that the "true doctrine" of "the law of nature, and the properties of the body politic" would be insinuated, taught, and otherwise instilled into the gifted youth of England who would "receive" it and "afterward teach it to the people" by every means at their command.

A further point. Unlike the rhetoric of theology or of classical political philosophy or heroic poetry, the rhetoric of Hobbes is itself ideally suited to the task. It is, above all, neutral. Men presumably do not come to blows over geometrical theorems. (This is a judgment whose optimism, incidentally, Hobbes was to have reason to question during his own lifetime, when he was knocked from pillar to post by some of the leading academic mathematicians of the time. He also did some knocking himself.) But at least theoretically to discuss politics henceforth would be to discuss geometry. "The skill of making and maintaining Commonwealths consisteth in certain rules, as doth arithmetic and geometry." To discuss politics is to become objective and remote, a neutral observer rather than a heated disputant. We witness in the disciplined austerity of academic political, social, and historical studies today similar tendencies, but with this significant difference: the academic scientist is not always aware of what exactly has been sacrificed. But Hobbes knew.

The state of war between nature and reason is reflected in a war between two lexicons representing the adversaries. There exists a perennial antagonism between fancies, imaginings, and passions expressed in metaphor, poetry, and other imprecise and extravagant modes of speech, and their adversary, discourse, a name given by Hobbes to the language of scientific reason. Rational scientific discourse must seek always to still the terrible and insistent voices of the inner self. We must study ourselves in order to disarm ourselves; must investigate ourselves, not as with Freud so we may choose by learning how to listen; the self in Hobbes' system is overcome by learning how *not* to listen. Hobbes' argument becomes as a charm to prevent us from falling victim to our passions. He keeps us "employed" with an incessant structuring of the world within and about us. We structure ourselves, our speech, our thoughts, our society, our politics in such a manner that the destructive passions will, insofar as possible, "faint and languish."

The key to the success of the enterprise is found in language. For language is no instinct, but the invention of human beings. It follows then that truth and falsity are attributes of language, not of nature. The hope resides with the capacity first, to achieve correct propositions and second, to deprive our words of their power to kindle strong passions. Because they can accomplish many ends, words are the threat, and at the same time the ultimate source of salvation. Since only man can reason, and because reason depends upon the prior capacity to use words, only man is capable of absurdity, romance, fiction, and superstition. But since rational man alone is the inventor of words that are prior even to reason, he has the means to correct definitions, he can overcome absurdity, abolish romance, withdraw attention from fiction, scorn superstition and all the other engines of the Kingdom of Darknesse.

The true end of civilized discourse is conditional knowledge set forth in an orderly, coherent fashion—namely, scientific expression. Viewed in this light, the only possible alternative to science is madness, with its preference for

chaos and the disordered expression of the passions un-
controlled. Science finds no ally in the evidences of madness: fancy, metaphor, and poetry.* Science demands pre-
cision, science demands judgment.

The aim of Hobbes' teaching is to shackle the extravagance of passion to science, to combat the language of
passion with discourse, and to quiet the inner Babel by
public order cast back upon the internal man. "There is
nothing I distrust more," Hobbes wrote in the concluding
pages of *Leviathan*, "than my own Elocution." That is no
doubt true. Yet he dared hope by means of that Elocution
to put an end to all forms of elocution, save the single one
of rational, denatured, abstract science, a gift worthy indeed of Prometheus.

Thus, at long last, was the work that Hobbes had taken
up with the strength of his mind and the might of his pen
finished.

He created an artificial world; with laws for binding
twine created he it. And he looked upon it and saw that
it was good.

And he created an artificial man; with an external conscience created he him. And he looked upon this thing and
saw that it also was good.

And he bound them up together, the artificial man to
the artificial world; their existences he bound up together,
so that if one should die, the other must surely die.

---

*This is the conclusion not of the ascetic or the pedant. Hobbes loved heroic
poetry enough to be sorely tempted, just as Plato himself was tempted by the
muse he most dreaded and loved. Hobbes' first literary project was a translation
of Homer. He composed an autobiography in verse. And at his death he was
engaged in a new translation of Homer's epics.

And he cut down the Tree of the Knowledge of Good and Evil that had stood in the garden, so that man would have no longer need to fear; but neither had he to hope, or to love.

And the great God of Political Geometry smiled, and spoke:

"*Ecce* . . . Behold *Leviathan!*"

Chapter 4

Rousseau's *Social Contract*: Politics as an Unnatural Act

> If to put oneself first is an inclination natural to man, and the first sentiment of justice is moreover inborn in the human heart, let those who say man is a simple creature remove these contradictions.
> Rousseau, *Émile*

R OUSSEAU spent a lifetime analyzing the contradictions endemic to humanity, man's towering egoism as well as his astonishing capacity for selflessness. At his best Rousseau came close to living the contradictions; he surely respected them; but like the rest of us, when from time to time the contradictions grew unbearable, he himself sought to remove them. In his pages natural man would often run roughshod over social custom and trample it. But there were other times when society would cut man to cloth of its own design. Here, the anarchist in Rousseau would assert itself, there, the pious defender of the civic religion. Occasionally, he would actually induce them to go together, hand in hand.

First a look at Rousseau in all his civic fury. "It is education," he wrote in *Considerations on the Government of Poland*, "that must give souls a national formation, and direct their opinions and tastes in such a way that they will be patriotic by inclination, by passion, by necessity." Unlike Hobbes, who meant to still the passions, Rousseau seeks to place them at the service of the state. Moreover, citizens must be accustomed "at an early age to rules, to equality, to fraternity, to competition, to living under the eyes of their fellow-citizens and to desiring public approbation." What this entails "is to arrange things so that every citizen will feel himself to be constantly under the public eye . . . [and] be so dependent on public esteem that nothing can be done, nothing acquired, no success obtained without it." Here we have Rousseau as champion of the civic version of the all-seeing One, the camera God in the guise of public judgment.

Even in that beautiful work where Rousseau achieves in words the rare synthesis of man and fellow-man he strove so hard to achieve in reality, even in *Émile* he is sometimes tempted to grant all to the citizen and nothing to the man. "The natural man lives for himself; he is the unit, the whole, dependent only on himself." But the citizen is the creation of a higher genius. He is "a numerator of a fraction, whose value depends upon the whole, that is, on the community. Good social institutions are those best fitted to make a man unnatural, to exchange his independence for dependence, to merge the unit in the group, so that he no longer regards himself as one, but as part of the whole, and is only conscious of the common life." Natural man appears but a genetic sport with no prior claims whatever upon society. "He who would preserve the supremacy of natural feelings in social life knows not what he asks. Ever at war with himself, hesitating between his wishes and his duties, he will be neither a man nor a citizen."

Rousseau—scourge of the natural man, destroyer of instincts, manufacturer of citizen-puppets. "Good social institutions are those best fitted to make a man *unnatural*." Those social institutions are best which succeed in "de-naturalizing" us. We forget our mother and our father and submit to the civil parent of us all; we forsake our brother for our brothers; we withdraw our membership in the natural tribe for membership in the political community. This is Rousseau's way of describing, and abetting, man's gradual rise from nature to human nature, the inexorable march of mankind in search of its own humanity. From the beginning, when Adam and Eve discerned their difference from the beasts, man has been in pursuit of his humanity. From the time he first rose upon his hind legs and found himself a freak among the creatures of Earth, man has sought his destiny as a being apart. Good social institutions are those designed to further this search. We humans, we unfinished ones, need civil society to discover our own true nature, to complete our being as creatures apart. We the God-like, created in His own image, need a laboratory to experiment with our own possibilities. Rousseau appears intent upon fashioning such a laboratory.

Yet at the same time Rousseau could fill scores of pages directed not only at preserving the natural sentiments, but even at returning them to supremacy within society itself. Social man is but a degenerate natural man, he would insist, a creature of straw, scarcely to be reckoned with at all. He is a deceit and a shame to all humanity, and Rousseau despises him. The natural man lives within himself alone. But "social man," Rousseau wrote in *A Discourse on the Origin of Inequality*, "lives constantly outside himself, and only knows how to live in the opinions of others, so that he seems to receive the consciousness of his own existence merely from the judgment of others concerning him." Pity Rousseau was not privileged to have at his disposal the results of nearly a century of social scientific investigation. For then he might even have found a more precise vocabulary to describe these ideal types, the natural and the social man. The one is "inner-directed" and the other, well, sort of "other-directed." Social man is the wretch and scandal of the universe. He has succeeded in reducing everything "to appearances, there is but art and mummery in even honour, friendship, virtue, and often vice itself." We are forever "asking others what we are, and never daring to ask ourselves, in the midst of such philosophy, humanity, and civilization, and of such sublime codes of morality, we have nothing to show for ourselves but a frivolous and deceitful appearance, honour without virtue, reason without wisdom, and pleasure without happiness." Mankind's greatest catastrophe was the fall into society. Civilization does indeed have its discontents.

The remedy for such a state of affairs seems plain enough: we must restore the natural man, we must dismantle the fake creature we have made, we must strip away the masks from our faces and stop the lies in our mouths. Death to the traitor, death to the social fiction, the mechanical man! All hail the return of Adam, hail the virile hero, the natural man who lives within himself! And yet—*néanmoins*. No sooner has he demonstrated man's one true destiny, than Rousseau witnesses that very creature fading from sight and turns to his alter ego to lend him substance.

Rousseau had written: "let those who say man is a simple creature remove [his] contradictions." It is obvious that from time to time Rousseau was bent precisely upon that attempt, now in behalf of the natural, now in behalf of the civilized man. But not always. Sometimes he was trying to instruct us in what it is like to live in contradiction, and how to maintain the contradictions without having them tear us apart. A career suited to the arts of a moral juggler, but an honest one, performing his daring act in the town square at high noon.

Where to begin? Geneva, Rousseau a lad of sixteen, in his words in *The Confessions,* "uneasy, discontented with myself and everything that surrounded me; displeased with my occupation, without enjoying the pleasures common to my age, weeping without a cause, sighing I knew not why, and fond of my chimerical ideas for want of more valuable realities." A typical adolescent in that he clung jealously to his fantasies, never mind the dictates of reality. Rousseau, however, deliberately chooses the former, and having the genius and courage to impress these fantasies upon reality itself, he set forth to change the world. Were the world impervious to the fantasies of Rousseau, perhaps our own history might be otherwise than it is.

How Rousseau set out to change the world he himself tells us in a sublime and terrible passage immediately following the description of his inner life during adolescence.

"Every Sunday, after sermon-time, my companions came to fetch me out, wishing me to partake of their diversions. I would willingly have been excused, but when once engaged in amusement, I was more animated and enterprising than any of them; it was equally difficult to engage or restrain me: indeed, this was ever a leading trait in my character." It was *equally difficult* to engage Rousseau or restrain him—speak of contradictions! "In our country walks I was ever foremost, and never thought of returning till reminded by some of my companions." Jean-Jacques was apprenticed at the time, and

was twice obliged to be from my master's the whole night, the city gates having been shut before I could reach them. The reader may imagine what treatment this procured me the following mornings; [custom prescribed a sound beating] but I was promised such a reception for the third, that I made a firm resolution never to expose myself to the danger of it. Notwithstanding my determination, I repeated this dreaded transgression, my vigilance having been rendered useless by a cursed captain, named M. Minutoli, who, when on guard, always shut the gate he had charge of an hour before the usual time. I was returning home with my two companions, and I got within half a league of the city, when I heard them beat the tattoo; I redouble my pace, I run with my utmost speed, I approach the bridge, see the soldiers already at their posts, I call out to them in a suffocated voice—it is too late; I am twenty paces from the guard, the first bridge is

already drawn up, and I tremble to see those terrible horns advanced in the air which announce the
fatal and inevitable destiny, which from this moment began to pursue me.

The alienation of modern man, announced by the blaring of the trumpet: Judgment Day. An unforgettable figure, irresistible to the novelist in Rousseau. No matter that
he took liberties with the materials or that his memory was
not the most reliable in the world. The figure itself arrests
us and remains impressed upon our political imagination.
Rousseau could not bring himself to return to Geneva the
next morning. Counting what he had forsaken by having
become an exile, Rousseau's lament is worthy of an Achilles.
"In my native country, in the bosom of my religion, family,
and friends, I should have passed a calm and peaceful life
in the uniformity of a pleasing occupation, and among con-
nections dear to my heart. I should have been a good
Christian, a good citizen, a good friend, a good man." Alas,
had only Jean-Jacques been a good boy. Had he returned
on time to Geneva, he might even have "passed a life of
happy obscurity." Instead of happy obscurity, what? Poor
Rousseau, condemned to a life of miserable celebrity. The
two paths, one to obscure community, the other to celebrated alienation, haunted Rousseau all his life. So especially did the question, might it not be possible to have
them both: to gain liberty, yet retain community; to blend
publicity with privacy; to lead a normal, yet creative existence; to cultivate the social man and still not uproot the
natural man within; to pass a life of extraordinary ordi-
nariness?

The City for Rousseau radiates warmth, but at a distance. The actual incidents he describes suggest mostly terror. At the gate stands the captain, implacable Authority, taking sadistic pleasure in the humiliation of a sensitive boy. Inside the walls waits the master, and inevitable punishment. The moat, the raised bridge, the horror of suffocation, the awful beating drums and blaring horns put an end to the citizen in young Rousseau that fear-laden night. "I threw myself on the [slope] in a transport of despair." Then came freedom but also loneliness, adventure but also statelessness, political philosophy but also political impotence, finally insanity.

I mention these things not to subject Rousseau or his writings to crude psychologizing, to argue that the man's political theory merely reflects or is a cover for an unhappy childhood—whatever that is. I mean rather to suggest that the formal concerns of Rousseau's political theory are also intensely personal concerns. To miss this relationship is to miss a significant dimension present in all powerful political thinking. For the genius of all great political thinkers is to make public that which is of private concern, to translate into public language the more special, idiosyncratic vocabulary of the inner man in hopes of arriving at public solutions which might then be internalized by each of us. One sure test of the quality of a political theory is its universality, that is, the extent to which everyman responds to the statement of problems which originated, perhaps, as the vexations of a single soul. The great thinker, in other words, suffers the malaise common to an age and possesses the courage and the craft to translate that malaise into a public vocabulary, in the hope of discovering political remedies for what had previously been thought private ills.

To return to Rousseau's tale of his own (metaphorical) alienation, how does one reconcile days inside the walls, in the warm sunlight, with long nights outside, in the cold loneliness, but where the muses often await one; communal life with freedom of spirit; sociability with the dark, guarded recesses of the soul?

Rousseau attempted to do so by a politics of compassion, with the power first to create citizens and then to turn them into comrades. My plan is to examine Rousseau's natural man, to determine what we carry with us into the city at the outset; and then to assess his scheme for establishing "a form of association which will defend and protect with the whole common force the person and goods of each associate, and in which each, while uniting himself with all, may still obey himself alone, and remain as free as before." May the wilderness coexist with civilization, or must one fall to the primacy of the other? May men live in society and also within themselves, or must the interior world be tamed and socialized lest the society they live in become a replica of the inner landscape—uncultivated, undomesticated, wild, unique? It is the *reconciliation of contradictions* we are addressing. And in reconciling contradictions, to listen to one voice only is not to be reconciled but solaced, that is, to be confirmed in our existing beliefs or else to be outraged, it makes little difference. Solace assumes now one, now the other guise. But to heed the inner voice while acting midst the hubbub of social life, to entertain questions of social justice while taking our own private pleasure, demands reconciliation. Rousseau taxes us to the breaking point, his words are a constant reminder of our suffering and our delight, not in isolation one from the other, but in a characteristic human mixture. His natural man and his social man are but fictions, metaphors permitting him, and us, to appreciate what is politically at stake in the contrariness of the unique human mix.

Rousseau's temptation to ally himself with culture and to reconstruct the nature of man, we have already witnessed in *Considerations on the Government of Poland* and *Émile*. For his temptation to ally himself with instinctual human nature and to purge society itself of its conceits, we must rely principally upon *The Discourses*, particularly *On the Arts and Sciences*, and *On the Origin of Inequality*. And for Rousseau at his best and most complex, the artist obsessed with the terrible problem of reconciling man and culture, we have *The Social Contract*.

I

Nature, the rude hearth of field and forest, the abiding home of man. Nature, which had for millennia shielded her children from the accursed knowledge of good and evil. Nature, source of all that is eternal, despoiled by Culture, bearer of that which is futile and debased in human existence. "Let men learn for once," Rousseau writes in *A Discourse on the Arts and Sciences*, "that nature would have preserved them from science, as a mother snatches a dangerous weapon from the hands of her child. Let them know that all the secrets she hides are so many evils from which she protects them. . . . Men are perverse; but they would have been far worse, if they had had the misfortune to be born learned."

Man is born ignorant of culture, at one with the nature about him, until the process of corruption we call education is imposed upon him by his elders. With time, which in human terms means nothing less than the grand march of the arts and sciences, and of religion, the true nature of humanity had been distorted almost beyond recognition. What to moderns must appear "natural" is as far from genuine human nature as the domesticated cat is from her jungle cousins. By the conceits of polite society men had been made into caricatures of themselves. To Rousseau nature is not simply twice blessed; she is blessed full sevenfold, and the fall of man into civilization is a tragedy fully seven times over. Let us examine those blessings, and that tragedy.

First Blessing: Nature had sustained and abetted manliness.

First Tragedy: Society, by deposing nature, has introduced femininity, and even effeminacy, as the ruling principle among mankind.

"Let the famous Voltaire tell us how many nervous and masculine beauties he has sacrificed to our false delicacy, and how much that is great and noble, that spirit of gallantry, which delights in what is frivolous and petty, has cost him." Throughout Rousseau's discussion of the fall of man from nature the theme of sacrifice is uppermost, the cost to humanity of acquiring culture. No less than the very nature of man is yielded up as the price for his continued existence as a civilized creature. Hobbes had demanded of men their particularities: Rousseau laments that sacrifice. The man has been sacrificed to the spaniel; "application to the sciences tends rather to make men effeminate and cowardly than resolute and vigorous."

Man is by nature a self-reliant creature. By creating culture, or rather by having been duped into becoming its ally, he has unwittingly contrived to emasculate himself. Curiously, Rousseau's natural man bears a striking resemblance to the warrior, and his natural state to the fraternity of the Achaeans on the plains of Troy, or of ancient Sparta. The passing of the rough justice and the rollicking friendship of comrades-in-arms occasions much regret in his pages. In such primitive organizations, antedating the civilizing gifts of the arts and sciences, men were not "so wealthy as to be enervated by effeminacy, and thence to lose, in the pursuit of frivolous pleasures, the taste for real happiness and solid virtue." In the warrior-state the real man is the most precious good; but Athens, "always learned always voluptuous, and always a slave," always murders her Socrates who was, after all, not a mere cloistered philosopher but a warrior and leader of men. To the sorrow of real men everywhere, Sparta has been increasingly subdued by Athens.

It has always been "thus with man," according to Rousseau in *A Discourse on the Origin of Inequality*, "as he becomes sociable and a slave, he grows weak, timid, and servile; his effeminate way of life totally enervates his strength and courage." Sociability, it would seem, dries up the precious bodily fluids. By the time of Rousseau, society had achieved a true prodigy, the subjection of the strong by the weak, which is a cruel reversal of the plan of nature.

And it was women and womanish men who were to blame. "It is easy to see that the moral part of love [between] the sexes is a factitious feeling, born of social usage, and enhanced by the women with much care and cleverness, to establish their empire, and put in power the sex which ought to obey."

Now, there is about all this a dread of sociability, a preoccupation with the loss of manhood in civilized society, and an awful fear of the disappearance of male dominance. The argument was given colorful expression by Nietzsche, who wrote that the free man "spits on the contemptible type of well-being dreamed of by shopkeepers, Christians, cows, females, Englishmen, and other democrats. The free man is a warrior." In the more recent words of D. H. Lawrence, "Unless a man believes in himself and his gods genuinely . . . his woman will destroy him. Woman is the nemesis of doubting man. She can't help it."

The fear of women has been a constant refrain in the history of political theory since Plato's caricature of Xanthippe and reverence for Sparta. Women and womanish men are disparaged again and again as the inventors of complex manners, of all varieties of social games, in a word, of culture; man is the silent warrior ensnared by women ("society") and unmanned. Such notions crop up especially in the thought of those who regard their own societies with contempt. Rousseau was certainly a member of the Brotherhood.

Second Blessing: The state of nature was hospitable to peace.

Second Tragedy: When men fell from nature they fell into mutual hostility. Far from being the condition of

peaceful existence, civilization makes warfare inevitable.
Which is a symmetrical reversal of Hobbes.

Paradoxical though it might sound, the natural warrior
was actually a creature of peace who fought only when provoked, and then only for his freedom, his honor, or his
mate; and the state of nature was distinguished by an absence of futile wars. It is rather the fearful civilized man,
the debased and snivelling product of society, who blusters
and clowns his way to destruction.

The culprit turns out in the end to be the institution
of private property. From modest, men became extravagant, from magnanimous, they became avaricious. Cries of
"natural compassion" were soon "suppressed," and "perpetual conflicts" became the order of the day. "The new-
born state of society thus gave rise to a horrible state of
war; men thus harassed and depraved were no longer capable of retracing their steps or renouncing the fatal acquisitions they had made." The acquisitions, of course,
were all sham: property, title, family, and religion.

Third Blessing: Nature is the fount of common sense.

Third Tragedy: By creating society men guaranteed the
triumph of sophistical reason.

"What is philosophy?" Rousseau asks. "What is contained in the writings of the most celebrated philosophers?" His answer is a sardonic masterpiece:

> To hear them, should we not take them for so many
> mountebanks, exhibiting themselves in public, and
> crying out, *Here, Here, come to me, I am the only
> true doctor?* One of them teaches that there is no
> such thing as matter, but that everything exists only

in representation. Another declares that there is no other substance than matter, and no other God than the world itself. A third tells you that there are no such things as virtue and vice, and that moral good and evil are chimeras, while a fourth informs you that men are only beasts of prey, and may conscientiously devour one another. Why, my great philosophers, do you not reserve these wise and profitable lessons for your friends and children? You would soon reap the benefit of them.

Nature is never foolish, only men are fools. Nature is never extravagant or pompous, only men are capable of extravagance and pomposity. When in touch with their own true natures, men speak with the plain tongue of common sense; the fall from nature, then, has also been a fall into metaphysical double-talk. And to think that Rousseau was writing well before the dawn of German scholarship.

Fourth Blessing: Not only is nature the fount of common sense, she is the source of truth.

Fourth Tragedy: Not only is society the patron of sophistical reason, she is the inventor of lying.

All educated and sociable men are "liars," sometimes despite themselves. But nature "never lies. All that comes from her will be true." Abstract language is the parent of deceit, art the elevation of lying to its highest form. Nature sometimes dissembles for the sake of survival. But the very principle of civilized society is dissembling, and it is sustained by the political relations established among men. The civilized creature "pays his court to men in power, whom he hates, and to the wealthy, whom he despises; he stops at nothing to have the honour of serving them." And those with the most power command the largest train of liars, be they legal counselors, poets, scientists, theologians, or philosophers.

Fifth Blessing: Nature is the repository of all that is healthful and sane.

Fifth Tragedy: Civilization appeared to hold the promise of maintaining that condition, while increasing the awareness of men, at the same time augmenting the goods available to them. Instead, the chief gifts of civilization have been depravity and disease:

> If she [nature] destined man to be healthy, I venture to declare that a state of reflection is a state contrary to nature, and that a thinking man is a depraved animal. When we think of the good constitution of the savages, at least of those whom we have not ruined with our spirituous liquors, and reflect that they are troubled with hardly any disorders, save wounds and old age, we are tempted to believe that, in following the history of civil society, we shall be telling also that of human sickness.

The history of civilization has been the history of human pathology. Civilization has not merely its discontents, but its neuroses. Men have brought upon themselves more diseases than medicine may hope to cure. In the civilized condition Rousseau locates diseases of idleness and also excessive labor, of exquisite foods and unwholesome foods, of fatigue, mental exhaustion, and the "anxieties inseparable from every condition of life" in society, by which "the

mind of man is incessantly tormented." When we purchased civilization, we purchased not only disease but
dread as well.

Sixth Blessing: By nature Rousseau understands, literally, reality. Men were once a part of that reality and in
themselves reflected an instinctual awareness of the whole.

Sixth Tragedy: Humanity relinquished its place in the
reality of the All, nature, and went to live in a house of
mirrors. Society is the capitol of appearance, a structure
erected entirely by men, and having no connection with
the rest of creation. Nor did men consult nature in the
shaping of their artificial universe.

So long as men dwelling in a state of nature had been
content to lead a simple and uncorrupted life, so long as
they were satisfied with rude clothing and rough shelter,
with bows and arrows and sharp-edged stones, with clumsy
fishing craft and crude musical instruments, there was no
need to value appearance over reality. For there existed
no envy, nor any lusting after place. But with the division
of labor and the rise of art and science and the coming of
a more sophisticated technology, the life of simple virtue
collapsed, and men became as we now know them. "It now
became the interest of men to appear what they really were
not. To be and to seem became two totally different things;
and from this distinction sprang insolent pomp and cheat-
ing trickery, with all the numerous vices that go in their
train." To be and to seem, two different things. Without
this distinction in practice, how could there be mere appearance? Without appearance, how could there exist pomp
and trickery? And in the absence of pomp and trickery, is
politics as we know it conceivable? For Rousseau politics

itself is but one of the "numerous vices that go in their train."

Seventh Blessing: A ruling principle of the natural order was that of compassion amongst human beings.

Seventh Tragedy: In society sophistication takes hold, and corrupts man's finest instinct by tempting him not merely to place his own interests always before the good of his fellows, but to rationalize and to justify such selfishness.

It is not nature but "philosophy" which, according to Rousseau, isolates man and "bids him say, at sight of the misfortunes of others: 'Perish if you will, I am secure.'" Such a finely civilized creature is able to retain his equanimity amidst the most awful suffering, provided of course that he himself is not the victim. "A murder may with impunity be committed under his window; he has only to put his hands to his ears and argue a little with himself, to prevent nature, which is shocked within him, from identifying itself with the unfortunate sufferer."

Uncivilized man has "not this admirable talent; and for want of reason and wisdom, is always foolishly ready to obey the first promptings of humanity." Thus it is from the most civilized nations, and from associations of men farthest removed from nature, that we may expect the most heartless, and "rational," atrocities. Since what Goethe would refer to as "the Era of Unselfish Crimes" was launched by the French Revolution, how refined the game has become.

The civilized are the creatures best schooled in preventing nature, shocked within them, from identifying with the pain of the unfortunate sufferer. Yet, as we shall soon see, however slim a reed this natural propensity of human beings to identify with the sufferings of others, it is Rousseau's chief hope for the establishment of a decent political community. After all, it does require enormous energy to stifle always the natural compassion we feel stirring within us.

Let us pause for a tally:

Nature	*Civilization*
Manliness	Effeminacy
Serenity	Wars of Destruction
Common Sense	Sophistry
Truth	Deceit
Health and Sanity	Depravity and Disease
Respect for Reality	Concern for Appearances
Compassion	Selfishness

Yet, I hope it is sufficiently clear that Rousseau speaks metaphorically: we ourselves are the bearers of *both* sets of tendencies within us, and the conflict rages; first one, then the other term to the dualism triumphs. The question is, can there be freedom without sacrificing man to his products, and peace without sacrificing culture to natural instinct? What is of continuing fascination is to witness the war being waged between nature and culture upon the battlefield of Rousseau's own soul.

In *The Confessions*, for instance, he admits puzzlement over "two things, very opposite . . . in me, and in a manner which I cannot myself conceive. My disposition is extremely ardent, my passions lively and impetuous, yet my ideas are produced slowly, with great embarrassment and after much afterthought. It might be said *my heart and understanding do not belong to the same individual.*" Rousseau described his passions as

> extremely violent; while under their influence, nothing can equal my impetuosity; I am an absolute stranger to discretion, respect, fear, or decorum; rude, saucy, violent, and intrepid: no shame can stop, no danger intimidate me. . . . [But] in my moments of tranquillity, I am indolence and timidity itself; a word to speak, the least trifle to perform, appear an intolerable labor; everything alarms and terrifies me; the very buzzing of a fly will make me shudder: I am so subdued by fear and shame, that I would gladly shield myself from mortal view.

This latter state becomes the basis later on for a melancholy irony, Rousseau's way of making a virtue of necessity. "I love society as much as any man," he writes, "was I not certain to exhibit myself in it, not only disadvantageously, but totally different from what I really am." But that's fine, really, in fact it couldn't be better. "The plan I have adopted of writing and retirement, is exactly what suits me. *Had I been present, my worth would never have been known, no one would ever have suspected it.*" Rousseau will recreate society in his imagination and deliver it in his writings, so that those who "love society" will not be compelled any longer to present themselves there as "totally different" from what they truly are.

How to bring the heart and the understanding together

in Rousseau? How to bring them together in every Rousseau, in every citizen, in all modern men? How to render unto Caesar that which is truly Caesar's and to God that which is rightfully His, without flying into bits? How to give to nature what belongs to nature, yet to divest oneself of one's own natural inclinations sufficiently to become also a creature of the human community? How to live in the city, yet still reside within oneself? How to offer up, only to receive in return, *oneself*, now enriched by convention, strengthened and refined by culture and morality, directed by laws and defended by civil liberties?

By his theoretical genius, Rousseau will make us free as before. Compassion is dead, long live compassion, long live the General Will, an invention of civilized man to replace the natural compassion sacrified in the fall from innocence, but which might yet be rekindled. The General Will is Rousseau's creation fashioned to stir nature, even within social artifice, to allow her sufficient freedom to experience shock once more by identifying with the cries of the unfortunate sufferer. By the General Will, the rational organization of compassion, men will from time to time at least experience that holy fraternity which was theirs before the calamity of civilized existence. By the General Will, which stirs compassion within the human soul, men will from time to time experience that heady freedom, that health and sanity, that oneness with all creation which, whether they had ever actually known it or not, they yearn to taste. Thus, while there is a metaphorical fall from innocence, there is no metaphorical redemption. All we might hope for are sporadic intimations of Paradise, kept alive by the civilized conscience.

The problem to be faced is monumental and, at the same time, superbly human. It is the identical one confronting Alice in Wonderland when, her fawn at her side, loving arm clasping the creature's neck, she departs the wood of forgetfulness for the plain of remembrance. At once child and beast grasp the mutual incompatibility of their separate destinies, the conventional alienation of their beings, and the fawn darts away in terror, abandoning the child-woman forever. What should be our reaction? Must we weep at the torment of our aloneness, or cry out for redemption?

Despite the opinions of many commentators, Rousseau does not advocate a return to the dark warm wood of forgetfulness. In *The Social Contract* he leads us resolutely out upon the plain of conscious thought, there to pitch our tents; and to see if we are capable of building in that place a city to which we will surrender up our deepest natures, only to receive them back now cleansed of certain of their imperfections and of their particularity. We offer up our own wild freedom, and receive in return the blessings of liberty. We hold nothing back—but yield up our very selves in hopes of receiving them once again, anointed by the sacrament of mutual pledging. But withal, conscious of our mortal limitations, and therefore of our inability ever to return to the blissful ignorance of innocence. The General Will becomes the externalization of natural conscience; our own world of internal games and of social appearances, the opposing principle. It is left ot us alone to make continuous adjustments to the requirements of the General Will. But on occasion, we must be forced to be free.

II

In *The Social Contract* we witness Rousseau the Village Sorcerer at his most brilliant, combining elements and reconciling opposites with astonishing dexterity. No wonder he is not always so easy to follow. He will, he tells us in the very first sentence, attend to men "as they are" and to "laws as they might be," and in the second he promises us the unity of right with interest and utility with justice. In *The Social Contract* Rousseau confronts, without shrinking, the age-old antagonisms between nature and culture.

"The constitution of man," Rousseau writes, "is the work of nature; that of the State the work of art. It is not in men's power to prolong their own lives; but it is for them to prolong as much as possible the life of the State, by giving it the best possible constitution." For Rousseau the best possible constitution is one which is able, by plumbing the depths of man's natural being, to tap his finest instincts and to mobilize them, by the art of Legislation, for the well-being of all. The Legislator must tap the instincts of man because what is common nature to all men has been corrupted by laws and customs and conventions. The task is one of enormous magnitude, a sort of psychological archaeology, a back-breaking expedition among the bones and shards of human nature.

In its gradual passage from a state of nature to a state of civilization, humanity underwent marked changes, perhaps the most striking of which was the substitution of morality, which is abstract and artificial, for instinct, which was reflexive and universal. This passage is, once again, metaphorical; that is, it applies equally to individual biography and to collective human development. Morality had no more place in nature than any other idea. Yet no society can endure without it. For having once impaired certain instincts and obliterated others, men need support in their search to relate once more to their fellows and to their environment. Morality is that invention of men which compels them to consult their intelligence before giving in to their—by now—corrupt inclinations. On balance, humanity has been the gainer. From a "stupid and unimaginative animal," the human has been made into "an intelligent being and a man." Yet only too often he has been debased beneath even his natural estate by bad laws and bad customs, by bad rulers and worse policies. Clearly, this statement is also metaphorical: Rousseau is not writing political history, he is seeking some persuasive way to relate internal nature with external culture. Rousseau hopes that by placing refined intelligence at the service of the community, man's nature may be enhanced by his art. What man *is* may be ennobled by what he can *make*, not least of all what he can make of himself.

First the tokens of natural freedom are to be cashed in for those of civil and moral liberty. "Each member of the community gives himself to it, at the moment of its foundation, just as he is, with all the resources at his command, including the goods he possesses." In return, he himself along with his freedom and all his goods are sent back to him, stamped LEGITIMATE. He gives up all only to receive all in return, now anointed by a mortal god, sanctified by the common authority and defended by the common force. Abraham gave his Isaac only to receive him back again, twice blessed as a gift of God. Rousseau's citizen also resigns everything that is most dear to him, and grasps everything again, by virtue of the creation of popular sovereignty. He resigns his very life. And he is reborn, now blessed by the secular god, the General Will. His life, Rousseau says, "is no longer a mere bounty of nature, but a gift made continuously by the state." As a result the citizen's "faculties are so stimulated and developed, his ideas so extended, his feelings so ennobled, and his whole soul so uplifted. . . . "

However free of religious conviction Rousseau himself might have been, the model by which he hopes to convince his readers of the efficacy of the General Will is resolutely religious. By a secular baptism men divest themselves of their accidental natures and assume a new identity as communal beings. Mere creaturehood is thus transformed into moral agency. The political community is to be founded, as the family is founded, on the sacrament of mutual giving. And the community is to be sustained, as the family is sustained, beyond the life of any single member. It is in this sense that it is meaningful to speak of the whole as being morally prior to, and greater than, the mere sum of its parts. For something *new* has come into the world, the political community, which is the most splendid creation of man as artist.

It is crucial to recognize, however, that Rousseau does not intend his citizen as a sacrifice to the state, although that is what he is likely to become, as I will show a bit later on; instead, he is to constitute its supreme authority. The citizen is to be more than the man, true enough, as the community is to be more than the citizen. But it is the expressed hope, at least, to have the General Will embody the spirit of the community, and the citizen to embody also the man. Rousseau enlists all of value in man which still lingers from a mythical prehistoric past, from primitive nature, particularly all which tends to fraternity and commonality, in order to maintain his state. At the same time he enlists the laws themselves in the struggle to bolster the constructive natural instincts against the inevitable corrosive influences of culture—of science, of art, and of polite society.

Whether it will all eventually work out precisely that way is another matter. It is Rousseau's expressed purpose I am addressing at the moment. "There are two kinds of dependence," he had written in *Émile*,

> dependence on things, which is the work of nature; and dependence on men, which is the work of society. Dependence on things, being non-moral, does no injury to liberty and begets no vices [that is, natural necessity is not demeaning]; dependence on men being out of order, gives rise to every kind of vice, and through this the master and slave become mutually depraved. If there is any cure for this social evil, it is to be found in the substitution of law for the individual, in arming the general will with a real strength beyond the power of any individual will. If the laws of nations, like the laws of nature, could never be broken by any human power, dependence on men would become dependence on things; *all the advantages of a state of nature would*

*be combined with all the advantages of social life
in the commonwealth* [my emphasis].

It is difficult to imagine a more impassioned defense of the
political community. As difficult as it would have been in
his earlier works, particularly the *Discourses*, to imagine
a more impassioned defense of the state of nature against
the wiles of society.

By the General Will all the advantages of a state of nature are to be combined with all those of civil society. And
the issue of such a blessed union is a man-citizen fierce and
unique in his individual character, yet compassionate and
gentle with his comrades. *Émile* presents us with an in-
triguing portrait of the ideal man-citizen. In educating such
a person, Rousseau did not desire to alienate him entirely
from the rich sources of his own nature, nor "to make him
a savage and . . . send him back to the woods, but [to make
sure] that living in the whirl of social life . . . he should not
let himself be carried away by the [ordinary] passions and
prejudices of men: let him see with his [own] eyes and feel
with his [own] heart," that is, combine the enlightened
eyes and heart with those of his natural being; combine
judgment with love, reason with compassion. Let him be
at once both man and citizen, both natural and conventional, both himself and what he—and Rousseau—have
made of him, a man truly at home in the city because he
bears his own, unique, landscape unimpaired within.

Whether this prodigy is actually accomplished in *The
Social Contract* is the next question: not whether the General Will works in reality, or whether it ever could, but
whether *it works in Rousseau's book*. My own, tentative,

conclusion is that perhaps for the Legislator, for the political theorist and founder of the State, it may. For the ordinary citizen, unfortunately, the promise of the General Will does not appear so bright. The Legislator might indeed see with his own eyes, the citizen through lenses ground to the specifications of the founder. The Legislator might feel with his own heart, the citizen more likely with a heart richly stocked with patriotic fervor and fraternal passion. Now given the political scene Rousseau described with such a sense of outrage in *The Discourses*, these achievements by themselves would be noteworthy moral advances—fervor in behalf of the community, rather than one's own material interests, and passion for the sufferings of one's comrades, rather than self-pity over one's own plight. But it still remains that the marvelous combination of instinct and awareness is to be expected less in the citizen than in the Legislator, whose inspired role I should like now to characterize as Rousseau sets it forth in *The Social Contract*.

III

Rousseau's state is a Republic, his citizens ardent Republicans. In the beginning, however, is the word, and the word belongs to the founder-god: Create. Rousseau cites with approval Montesquieu's dictum that "At the birth of societies, the rulers of Republics establish institutions, and afterwards the institutions mould the rulers." To Rousseau, Legislation is the most exalted of functions, for the Legislator who founds a Republic "nowhere enters into its constitution; it is an individual and superior function, which has nothing in common with human empire." Instead, Legislation is the province of a Lycurgus, a Solon, a Moses. And perhaps their more earthbound surrogates, the Machiavellis and the Hobbeses and the Rousseaus as well, despite Rousseau's disclaimer at the outset that he himself is no Legislator. "The great soul of the legislator is the only miracle that can prove his mission." To establish a Republic a founder is necessary; to create Republicans he must divest the people, much as Machiavelli does his Prince, of their previous natures, inclinations, loyalties, and beliefs, all of which had become corrupted in a corrupt commonwealth.

"He who dares to undertake the making of a people's institutions," Rousseau declares, "ought to feel himself capable, so to speak, of changing human nature, of transforming each individual, who is by himself a complete and solitary whole, into part of a greater whole from which he in a manner receives his life and being; of altering man's constitution for the purpose of strengthening it; and of substituting a partial and moral existence for the physical and independent existence nature has conferred on us all." Man is to be plucked from his fierce isolation and made into a moral agent. The Legislator must

> take away from man his own resources and give him instead new ones alien to him, and incapable of being made use of without the help of other men. The more completely these natural resources are annihilated, the greater and the more lasting are those which he acquires, and the more stable and

perfect the new institutions; so that if each citizen is nothing and can do nothing without the rest, and the resources acquired by the whole are equal or superior to the aggregate of the resources of all the individuals, it may be said that *legislation is at the highest possible point of perfection* [my emphasis].

The man must be alienated from himself, must become part of a whole which is the political community, and made into a citizen.

Rousseau seeks to excise our irascibility and our prideful self-destructiveness, then to subject us to the close warm bonds of fraternity. The people, he says, "submitting to the laws of the state as to those of nature [herself], and recognizing the same power in the formation of the city as in that of man, [will] obey freely, and bear with docility the yoke of the public happiness." To bear with docility the yoke of the public happiness: thus begins the peaceful repose inaugurated by the General Will.

The state thrives just so long as nature and convention are blended in harmony—in Rousseau's words, so long as "the natural relations are always in agreement with the laws on every point, and law only serves, so to speak, to assure, accompany, and rectify them." The State perishes when this harmony is disrupted. Then the laws begin to "lose their influence, the constitution will alter, and the state will have no rest from trouble till it is either destroyed or changed, and nature has resumed her invincible sway." Men are then left to choose: feral nature, or sterile culture.

What a superb irony! The trick, for the Legislator, is to create a seamless web of nature and art. Where he is unsuccessful, nature will surely reassert herself and consume the state. The steaming jungles encroach upon the city and crack open its walls. But where the Legislator actually succeeds, he himself hides from the eyes of the citizens his very accomplishment, as well as the means employed, in rendering them happier, and more docile. By the rules of the game he is disqualified from letting the rest of us in on his secret. Instead, he attempts to persuade us that it was eternal nature, rather than mortal man, which set the conditions for our social well-being.

In other words, the Legislator himself contributes not at all to the elementary political education of the citizens. They are not permitted, let alone encouraged, to discuss the basic curriculum or to participate in its formulation. Nor does he contribute to their heightened awareness of what is at stake in blending art and nature in the political order, or in choosing to be political at all. That risk he has already taken for them. By the constitution he prescribes, the Legislator indoctrinates the citizens in the rules and values he deems suitable for them, and in the political games and institutions pursuant to those rules and values.

Consider for a moment. Successful laws appear to the citizens not as laws framed by mere mortals for their own governance, but commands of nature or of God, having their origin in the One true source of all the laws of the universe. The indispensable condition of individual morality—the inner conflict between the demands of the juridical order and those of one's own being—is not met by Legislation, but is actively suppressed by the Legislator. Only the inspired founder of the constitution is privileged to experience that instructive conflict, and to have his moral imagination challenged. The conditions for political creativeness are established for the Legislator only; only he will taste political glory or, perhaps, simply miserable celebrity. As for the rest of us, well, from a state of unhappy obscurity we are carried to a state of happy obscurity. The genius of the Legislator remains intact, his delight taken in the god-like experience of preparing his people to receive the moral purgative of the General Will. Must it always end up that way?

There is a doubt, which is why my conclusions, or anybody else's, are scarcely a match for Rousseau's fertile political imagination. In *The Social Contract* he writes: Machiavelli "professed to teach kings; but it was the people he really taught. His *Prince* is the book of Republicans." It is not beyond all possibility that Rousseau professed to teach Legislators; but really it was the people he taught. Nor that his *Social Contract* is the book of Democrats. Is it impossible to believe that in *The Discourses* Rousseau was instructing us in what we do to *ourselves*? For it is *we* who continually resign our freedom; it is *we* who cannot tolerate living within ourselves; and it is *we* who demand the bread of society and of politics and the circuses of the arts and sciences. *The Discourses* hold up a mirror to the ways we have of divesting ourselves of our integrity as human beings.

By the same stretch of the imagination, is it not possible that in *The Social Contract* Rousseau was equally intent upon informing us of the designs our *rulers* have upon our liberty: how they have sought to persuade us that not *they themselves* created the laws, but God or nature; not *they* altered human nature, but the course of natural development; that not *they* desired our unnatural dependence upon the state, our patriotic fervor and love of civic religion? No one, we are told, wills these goods but *ourselves*, and we will them because they are natural to us and within the order of things in the universe. But were all this actually so, why the ardor of Rousseau to set up a Legislator removed from nature herself?

Whether in *The Discourses* Rousseau is describing our natural origins and our social fall, or pointing out how we continue to betray ourselves, I do not know. Whether in *The Social Contract* he is portraying our destiny, or telling a cautionary tale of the ways in which our leaders, often in the guise of democracy, shape our destiny for us, I do not know either. I know only this: that these are questions of the first magnitude for politics, and that no other modern political theorist has achieved the heights of refinement in posing them as has Rousseau. For it was Rousseau's genius, and his fate, to be at the same time one of the last of the solacers and the first of the unmaskers of the machinery of solace employed by the modern State.

Chapter 5

Political Theory Without Solace

I

THE nineteenth was an exuberant and cruel century, opening as it did with the promise of universal revolution and closing, in the Great War, with an end to hope for many who had seen in the doctrines of a hundred or so years a break with the benighted past. God had been put in His place, religions chastened, tyrants tweaked, the nation-state, grown fat and stupid with power, flayed by some of the bitterest and most brilliant pens in the West. The reconciliation of liberty and equality had, by mid-century, seemed imminent, inevitable almost, and an end to both the old slavery to superstition and the new bondage to the machine appeared near at hand. A century of disenchantment, of confident unmasking, would not fail to bring Liberation to those with the will to reach out for it (Nietzsche); as well as those destined to be the beneficiaries of an historical process overrunning impediments flung its way by mere human agency (Marx).

Equality, fraternity, liberty, utility, socialism, the transvaluation of all values and the dethronement of the Emperor of the Universe—what a prospect! Among the leading thinkers, tradition was either to be uprooted entirely, or to provide the soil out of which a glorious future would necessarily bloom. To this mood of optimism, cautious trumpeters of the new age like Sigmund Freud contributed by his method what he denied by his gloomy view of man's perennial struggle with both himself and his culture. Humanity was shaken at last from the metaphysical repose which had endured for millennia.

Kierkegaard, Marx, and Nietzsche stood, in the words of Hannah Arendt, "at the end of the tradition, just before the break came." They serve us, in this respect, as "guideposts to a past which has lost its authority. They were the first to think without the guidance of any authority whatever." From these remarks, one might expect Arendt to unloose a lament against the modern age. Instead, she makes this astonishing assertion: "In some respects," she says, "we are better off." The prophets of disenchantment presented us with an unparalleled gift, "the great chance to look upon the past with eyes undistracted by any tradition, with a directness which has disappeared from Occidental reading and hearing ever since Roman civilization submitted to the authority of Greek thought."*

At the same time Arendt notices about the intellectual upheavals of the nineteenth century something which has eluded all but the most astute commentators on the assault

---

*"Tradition and the Modern Age," in Arendt, *Between Past and Future* (1968), pp. 28-29.

upon traditional authority. "The destructive distortions of
the tradition," she writes, "were all caused by men who
had experienced something new which they tried almost
instantaneously to overcome and resolve into something
old." Columbus insisted that he had discovered no New
World, but merely a trade route to the Indies; Newton
merely stood upon "the shoulders of giants"; the Founders
of the United States Constitution merely encoded "American experience," rather than establishing a novel system
of government. Each of the unmaskers in the nineteenth
century had performed a prodigious leap into the past, only
to demonstrate thereby that the past was inadequate to his
purposes.

Kierkegaard's somersault, for example, was a leap from
doubt into belief, a "reversal" and a "distortion" of the traditional way of regarding the "relationship between reason
and faith." Marx's leap from "theory into action," and from
"contemplation into labor," served in practice what Hegel
had sought to accomplish in philosophy, the transformation
of metaphysics into a theory of history. Nietzsche's leap
from the "transcendent realm of ideas" into the "serious-
ness of life" constituted the "last attempt to turn away from
the tradition, and it succeeded only in turning tradition
upside down." Nietzsche's transvaluation of all values led
him, not into the future, but backwards into an "inverted
Platonism." Thus was the wound opened between thought
and action, with the consequent loss of coherence, of
meaning in strictly human terms. The tradition of political
theory in the West had begun with Plato's discovery that
it is "inherent in the philosophic experience to turn away
from the common world of human affairs; it ended when

nothing was left of this experience but the opposition of thinking and acting, which, depriving thought of reality and action of sense, makes both meaningless."*

Our Liberators, intending precisely the opposite, plunged us back into the past, only consigned no longer to the care of authorities, however personally ambitious or negligent of our fortunes, but naked, stripped of all meaning, our lives adrift. We find ourselves back in political and psychological time before Machiavelli and Hobbes and Rousseau, deprived of the solace of mystery, authority, or preordained destiny, alone, groping our way through a labyrinth of uncertainty.

Elsewhere, Arendt notes that not only has the "whole structure of Western culture come toppling down over our heads," but that we now find ourselves pervaded by "a fundamental distrust of everything merely *given*." This compels us

> not only to find and devise new laws, but to find and devise their very measure, the yardstick of good and evil, the principle of their source. . . . Politically, this means that before drawing up the constitution of a new body politic, we shall have to create—not merely discover—a new foundation for human community as such.

If not, the very earth itself will perish, "an event which will leave the sublime indifference of nature untroubled."†

---

*Arendt, pp. 29, 25.
†*The Origins of Totalitarianism* (1951), pp. 434-36.

I reproduce Arendt's diagnosis less for its authority than as a representation of the thought of some of the best minds on the subject of modernity. Besides, writing on this matter, she employs a language free of Existentialist obscurantism on the one hand, and Marxist jargon on the other. For there does exist at present an opposition of thinking and acting driving to the edge of madness those of us unfortunate enough not to escape a sense of obligation to act politically in the world. Most people, according to George Orwell, wish desperately to believe that "every choice, even every political choice, is between good and evil, that if a thing is necessary it is also right." But all such beliefs belong "to the nursery." To the mature mind it has become all too obvious that in politics "there are some situations which one may only escape by acting like a devil or a lunatic."* That is, taking political action today must often mean taking leave of one's senses. Such thinkers as Kierkegaard and Marx and Darwin and Freud and Nietzsche could scarcely have intended to turn us into a race of devils and lunatics, the condition presumably in which they found us. But once depart the known shore, however ugly, for the unknown, and we find ourselves adrift without a compass. There is little of solace in such an image. As for the absence of standards upon which to base any action whatever, the words of Albert Camus are characteristically to the point: "Can man alone create his own values? That is the whole problem."†

---

*"Writers and Leviathan" (1948), in S. Orwell and I. Angus, eds., *The Collected Essays, Journalism and Letters of George Orwell* (1968), Vol. IV, p. 413.

†*Notebooks, 1942-1951*, translated and annotated by J. O'Brien (1966), 1944, p. 94.

Arendt, Orwell, Camus—all are champions of a political theory free of solace, each is the writer as hero in our time. No matter that one or another sometimes loses the vision to which each holds tight in a bewildering and dangerous world. The point is that all of them grasp with remarkable clarity the temptations of the political thinker in the contemporary age, and each builds his thought around political events experienced as you and I experience only our profoundest loves and despairs in our private lives. Finally, each winds up appealing for limitations upon the ambitions and resentments of humanity, should there be any chance for our survival, let alone prospects for our living with dignity and mutual respect.

For George Orwell the Spanish Civil War, during which he took a sniper's bullet in the throat, was the decisive public event of his life. True, there had been his early hitch in the British Imperial forces in Burma, an episode he would grow to loathe—but out of which would come some of his most striking observations—as well as his disappointment with English socialist politics and politicians by 1935, when it had become·clear, at least for those who wished to see, that despotism had remorselessly crushed the revolutionary spirit in the Soviet Union. Still, it was the shattering experience of having been pressed on one side by Franco's Falangist troops and hounded on the other by Communists in Spain, those he had naively expected to number among his allies, which stripped Orwell of any possible comfort in fighting for the "right" cause. "The way things are going in Spain simply desolates me," he wrote to Stephen Spender in 1938.* Uncritical ideology

---

*Orwell and Angus, Vol. I, p. 312.

everywhere distorted plain facts and encouraged murder on the vastest scale as the superpowers watched Spain, girding themselves for the bloody test of the Second Great War. An unthinking conformity, which he was to take to monstrous lengths in *1984*, threatened to still the voice of critical reason; what Orwell wished above all to hear amidst the clamorous preparations for war was a single genuine "human voice" instead of "fifty thousand gramophones . . . playing the same tune"*

Even after that war had ceased raining its devastation upon humanity, George Orwell was busy contesting the devil and the lunatic striving within political actors, both grand and modest. One simply has got to resist the temptation to borrow weapons from the arsenals of one's enemies, however cruel and devious. "I always disagree . . . when people end by saying that we can only combat Communism, Fascism or what not if we develop an equal fanaticism. It appears to me that one defeats the fanatic precisely by *not* being a fanatic oneself, but on the contrary by using one's intelligence."† If Orwell, after all he had seen and suffered, could not play the devil or the madman in politics in order to feel free to act, he would still use his intelligence. But his was an intelligence, however suffused with compassion, which could resist the fatal romanticism of believing in ideas as "truths," even when those ideas were arrayed in behalf of his own ideology.

George Orwell was not a philosopher. He himself admitted on numerous occasions that he was not truly a nov-

---

*New English Weekly, September 1938, in *ibid.*, Vol. I, p. 351.
†To Richard Rees, 1949, in *ibid.*, Vol. IV, p. 478.

elist either, but a political writer. By "political" he meant
driven by the desire "to push the world in a certain direction, to alter other people's idea of the kind of society they
should strive after." In his view, no book is ever "genuinely
free from political bias." Even the opinion "that art should
have nothing to do with politics is itself a political attitude."*

His most notable claim upon us is as a political reporter
who by example (*The Road to Wigan Pier, Homage to Ca-
talonia*, as well as numerous essays, among them "Politics
and the English Language," "A Hanging," "Shooting an
Elephant") set the standards for political reporting on the
Left in the English-speaking world of the thirties and forties. He brought himself into touch with people in all walks
of life, and exhibited a special compassion for the poor and
for victims of any dehumanizing ideology, while himself
refusing to drown such compassion in sentimentality. Man
is man. He is not, as in the ideologies of those who saw a
special historical or spiritual destiny for this creature, "a
failed saint." The essence of being human is rather

> that one does not seek perfection, that one *is* some-
> times willing to commit sins for the sake of loyalty,
> that one does not push asceticism to the point
> where it makes friendly intercourse impossible, and
> that one is prepared in the end to be defeated and
> broken up by life, which is the inevitable price of
> fastening one's love upon other human individuals.

"Non-attachment" Orwell saw as a "desire to escape from

*"Why I Write" (1946), in *ibid.*, Vol. I, p. 4.

the pain of living, and above all from love, which, sexual or non-sexual, is hard work." One must choose between sainthood and humanity, "between God and man."* Orwell chose the unsolaced life, wagering upon no transcendent meaning other than the struggle, no reward other than the sharing of himself with friends and lovers as well as with the downtrodden, his comrades in the field.

Hannah Arendt has written that "thought itself arises out of incidents of living experience and must remain bound to them as the only guideposts by which to take its bearings."† Her living experience revolved about exile and the Holocaust, her chief preoccupations were the sources and manifestations of Evil besetting the modern condition. And Evil, which once she had thought "motivated," she now saw as unleashed upon the world in the twentieth century by no demonic powers such as we find, say, in certain of the characters of Dostoyevsky; rather the "sad truth of the matter is that most evil is done by people who never made up their mind to be either good or bad."‡ The chief casualty of the modern world has been human *judgment*. Wherever he goes, man encounters only himself; neither history nor nature is any help, they are scarcely conceivable any longer except as inventions or artifacts of humankind. In the absence of a common world capable at once of relating men and of keeping them apart, our alternatives appear lives of desperate loneliness, or existences con-

---

*"Reflections on Gandhi" (1949), in *ibid.*, vol. IV, p. 467.

†"Preface," *Between Past and Future*, p. 14.

‡In her remarkable piece, "Thinking and Moral Considerations: A Lecture" for W. H. Auden, *Social Research* (Autumn 1971), p. 438.

gealed into a mass, the heritance of human beings still vaguely related to one another in certain unsatisfying respects. In either case judgment has failed to survive the loss of a meaningful world which once people had shared in common.*

The crisis in philosophy and metaphysics—and political theory—was laid bare when "philosophers began to declare the end of philosophy and metaphysics" and political theorists proclaimed an end to "the Tradition" in political theory. It is not that God is dead, "an obvious absurdity in every respect," or that the traditional questions now appear "meaningless," but rather that the way God has been conceived in the West is no longer persuasive and the way traditional questions have been framed and responded to no longer promising, or even possible. By consigning a world transcending that of appearances to the scrapheap of history, mankind inadvertently destroyed the only world known through the senses. Once the "precarious balance between the two worlds is lost," according to Arendt, "no matter whether the 'true world' abolishes the 'apparent one' or vice versa, the whole framework of references, in which our thinking was used to orienting itself, breaks down. In these terms, *nothing seems to make much sense anymore.*"†

It is not the thirst for knowledge, for the satisfaction of which universities and industrial and governmental research institutes have been established and enriched all over the globe, but the quest for meaning which is at stake

---

*See "The Concept of History," in *Between Past and Future*, pp. 89-90.

†"Thinking and Moral Considerations," pp. 420, 421, n. 4, emphasis added.

in the contemporary world. The pursuit of knowledge, however, today feels "natural" and desirable, while thinking appears somehow "unnatural," as though human beings, "when they begin to think, engage in some activity contrary to the human condition." Thinking, unlike organized research, after all promises nothing; "like the veil of Penelope," thinking "undoes every morning what it had finished the night before." The "professional thinkers" of the past, to whose works we turn in order to pursue "the Tradition," had composed such works for those people, always in the majority, who wished "results" and could not care less about drawing "distinctions between knowing and thinking, between truth and meaning." The consequence has been that "few thinkers ever told us what made them think and even fewer still have cared to describe and examine their thinking experience."* We know more about more than ever: we think less about less than ever. No wonder judgment has become so damnable, even futile, an exercise. Hannah Arendt's perspective upon the present realities and future prospects of humanity is as bleak as that recorded a decade or two earlier by George Orwell. Her rejection of solace is equally determined.

Arendt's description of the evils which infest intellectual and political life in the West today is unrelieved. The following phrases are all Arendt's, cribbed from works spanning the years from 1951 until her death, selected and ordered to withhold, if only for a moment, her profoundest reactions to the horrors she portrays. The chief characteristic of political life today is "sheer insanity" (1951); tradi-

---

*Ibid., pp. 424-427.

POLITICAL THEORY WITHOUT SOLACE   137

tional culture "looks like a field of ruins" (1968); there exists "homelessness on an unprecedented scale, rootlessness to an unprecedented depth" (1951); wherever "paralysis of thought" is escaped at all, there remains at best but "perplexity for all" (1971, 1968); the "essential structure of all civilizations"—and not only that of the West— "is at the breaking point" (1951); the "fashionable search for identity is futile and our modern identity crisis could be resolved only by losing consciousness" (1971); finally, the belief that "everything is possible seems to have proved only that everything can be destroyed"(1951).

As was the case with Orwell—*1984* hardly began to approach the abominations which were later to come to light more fully in the archives of the thirties and forties and the events since his death in 1950—Arendt is remorseless in her repeated refusal of the solaced life. In 1951, concluding the Preface to *The Origins of Totalitarianism*, she writes:

> We can no longer afford to take that which was good in the past and simply call it our heritage, to discard the bad and simply think of it as a dead load which by itself time will bury in oblivion. The subterranean stream of Western tradition has finally come to the surface and usurped the dignity of our tradition. This is the reality in which we live. And this is why all efforts to escape from the grimness of the present into nostalgia for a still intact past, or into the anticipated oblivion of a better future, are vain.

We must confront the present on its own terms, without blinking. The reliance upon tradition leads at best to ambiguity, and the reliance upon dreams of a fabulous future leads to mindlessness. In 1968, in "What Is Freedom?," she extolls the virtue of courage to enter politics in any way, shape, or form whatever:

> It requires courage even to leave the protective security of our four walls and enter the public realm, not because of particular dangers which may lie in wait for us, but because we have arrived in a realm where the concern for life has lost its validity. Courage liberates men from their worry about life for the freedom of the world. Courage is indispensable because in politics not life but the world is at stake.*

Finally in 1971, in "Thinking and Moral Considerations," Arendt manages to rotate the considerations ever so slightly, but enough to remind us once again that thought "arises out of incidents of living experience and must remain bound to them as the only guideposts by which to take its bearings": she concludes her lecture by insisting that "The manifestation of the wind of thought is no knowledge; it is the ability to tell right from wrong, beautiful from ugly. And this indeed may prevent catastrophes, at least for myself, in the rare moments when the chips are down."† In this rare moment she feels compelled to take

---

*Between Past and Future, p. 156.

†"Thinking and Moral Considerations," concluding sentences, p. 446.

the reader behind the public façade of her *Eichmann in Jerusalem* to the personal-philosophical concern underlying her thesis of "the banality of evil" in that work: not glittering triumph, not even improvement, but the far more modest, though indispensable, concern to prevent "catastrophes." In this, Arendt, like Orwell, is of the company of Albert Camus, whose thought will now provide the material for an extended consideration of political theory without solace in the twentieth century.

II

The wife of a holy man had a quarrel with her serving girl. She accused the servant of having broken a dish, and demanded payment for the damage. The girl, on the other hand, denied the charge and refused to replace the article. The quarrel grew more and more heated. Finally, the wife of the holy man decided to refer the matter to a court of arbitration, and dressed quickly for a visit to the chief judge. When the holy man saw this, he, too, put on his best clothes and, in response to his wife's question, said that he intended accompanying her to court. She objected on the ground that it was not fitting for him to go with her; besides, she knew what to say to the judge. "You know it very well," the holy man said, "but the poor orphan, your servant, in whose behalf I am coming, does not know it, and who except me is there to defend her cause?"

Hassidic Tale

Today every intellectual and pseudo-intellectual, of whatever persuasion, is the master of such terms as "estrangement," "alienation," "rebellion," and of course "the

Absurd." Instead of beginning with Camus's philosophic vocabulary, attempting to define terms he has already given formal meaning in his essays, I propose to look at Camus as the modern political man struggling with a dreadful problem whose settlement means everything to him. His tortured pieces on the Algerian tragedy in *Resistance, Rebellion and Death* read like words addressed to the court in behalf of the falsely accused servant, the Arabs, and to the servant herself on behalf of the outraged wife, the French. My plan is to annotate those practical words with his theoretical discussions of justice and freedom in *The Myth of Sisyphus* and *The Rebel*. Thus I shall be interested far less in Camus's assessment of the specific political situation in Algeria, causes and prospects, than in the perspective he brings to any political situation in which he feels engaged. Whether Camus is "right" or "wrong" is not at issue. What is at issue is the relevance of his philosophic categories to political choices in the real world, a world devoid of enchantment, even of value.

In facing up to Algeria, Camus confronts the conflicting, often contradictory, demands represented by his attachments to his people and to his principles. The conflict is between one part of Camus, his "partiality" or "particularity," his flesh and blood existence as well as his personal history; and his "generality" or "universality," that part of him which reaches out beyond himself to clasp other men in friendship or to win for them justice or freedom, an extension of what he equally respects in himself, namely, his honor.

The predicament in which Camus found himself on the Algerian question was primarily a product of his own history. Following the Franco-Prussian War, Camus's Alsa-

tian grandparents had decided in favor of France, left their
native soil and taken up residence in Algeria. His father
had fought in the east of France in 1914, and his family had
once again rallied to the defense of the Republic in the
Second War. Camus had given himself to the French Resistance. Meanwhile, the Camus family had become Al-
gerians, regarding themselves first and foremost as citizens
of that land and giving no thought to emigration. Camus
himself, ironically, had been compelled to fight in France
proper rather than in North Africa because he had been
forced into exile earlier by the French rulers of Algeria, in
retaliation against his youthful attacks upon their inhuman-
ity toward the Arabs. His play *Caligula*, for instance, was
scarcely destined to win favor for him among the French
high command. Camus's was a working-class family, in his
words, "free of hatred," who had "never exploited or oppressed anyone," including their Arab neighbors. If you
happen to be a third-generation American and can imagine
yourself now being told, You, go back to Ireland where
your grandparents came from, or to Russia, Italy, England,
Japan, or Germany—then you can also appreciate Camus's
sorrow in contemplating the expulsion of his people from
Algeria. The political fact that Algeria, unlike the United
States, was a dependency is of no real human account. At
the same time, Camus felt not only a genuine affection for
the Algerian Arab and his culture, but a strong conviction
that the demands of the Arab for recovering "a life of dignity and freedom" were justified.

According to Camus the Arab objection to "Colonialism
and its abuses" was justified; the Arab outrage over the
"perennial lie of constantly proposed but never realized
assimilation, a lie that has compromised every evolution

since the establishment of Colonialism," was justified. Finally, enormous "psychological suffering: the often scornful
or offhand manner" displayed by too many French toward
them and the consequent feeling of "humiliation" had led
to the Arabs' militant demand for dignity as free men. In
this demand Camus thought the Arabs also justified.

We have now more than an inkling of the plot—the
drama is inescapable, the stage is set, the chief actors are
waiting in the wings. How to write the script, however, for
there are many turnings, how to resolve such explosive
contradictions and so many conflicting feelings and ideals?
One way, obviously, is by resignation, by condoning in-
justice and the torture of the Arabs; that is, by murder.
Here we see the theme of *The Rebel*. Is it ever justified
to commit political murder, whether by violence or by the
more subtle forms invented by civilized men? The question
posed in *The Rebel* is more than a metaphysical or aesthetic
one. An equally obvious way to resolve the Algerian business is by renunciation, by joining the guilt-ridden Parisian
who had never set foot upon North African soil in con-
demning his own people for withholding justice from the
Arabs; by leaving his people to their predictable fate at the
hands of the Arab nationalists; or by urging them to surrender all claims and accept self-imposed exile; that is, by
suicide. Here we see the theme of *The Myth of Sisyphus*.
The question posed in *Sisyphus* is more than a metaphysical or even a psychological one.* Camus rejects both responses to the Algerian crisis, murder and suicide:

---

*I am aware that *Sisyphus* was written in 1940. But in the "Preface" to the
Algerian Papers (1958) Camus writes that his "articles and texts" on Algeria were
"spaced out over a period of twenty years—from 1939, when almost no one in
France was interested . . . until 1958, when everyone talks about it."

The truth, alas, is that a part of French opinion vaguely holds that the Arabs have in a way earned the right to slaughter and mutilate while another part is willing to justify in a way all excesses [against the Arabs]. To justify himself, each relies on the other's crime. But that is a casuistry of blood, and it strikes me that an intellectual cannot become involved in it, unless he takes up arms himself. When violence answers violence in a growing frenzy that makes the simple language of reason impossible, the role of intellectuals cannot be, as we read every day, to excuse from a distance one of the violences and condemn the other. This has the double result of enraging the violent group that is condemned and encouraging to greater violence the violent group that is exonerated. If they do not join the combatants themselves, their role (less spectacular, to be sure!) must be merely to strive for pacification so that reason will again have a chance.

Camus views this dilemma as truly absurd, then chooses to live with it, day by day, year after year, however much it hurts. "Algeria," he wrote, "is the cause of my suffering . . . as others might say their chest is the cause of their suffering." Thus "I have lived through the Algerian calamity as a personal tragedy." And again, "We are pitted against each other (Arabs and French) condemned to inflicting the greatest possible pain on each other, inexpiably. The idea is intolerable to me and poisons each of my days."

To put it another way, the opposing demands of a fierce yet compassionate soul inflict pain on Camus, inexpiably.

That is what poisons his days. How he must have yearned, as we ourselves know full well from our own experience, to fall into bad faith and to urge the murder of the Arabs or the withdrawal of the French. Either course would have ended the agonizing contradictions. But to choose one alternative would have violated everything the man had written and everything his being stood for. He must resist the temptation to wield a bloody axe instead of a compassionate pen. That Camus the human being actually did often fall into bad faith is not surprising: the internal conflict was intense, the suffering awful.

So he chooses to live with the contradictions and try to mediate them: to retain diversity even while counseling unity; to struggle against totality, against laying the dilemma to rest by denying either party the right to exist with dignity. He lives in this fashion, day after day, for twenty years, without resignation, without renunciation, or hope either, for that matter, without romantic dreams of the magic solution or succumbing to the fantasy that the problem will simply disappear. He chooses to suffer with the dilemna and, whenever the occasion presents itself— as when an Arab friend should affirm their communion in brotherhood—rejoices with it. For it is a part of his life, and Camus will not deny himself by denying any part of the tragedy.

In portraying the absurd attitude, Camus once said that this type of "struggle implies a total absence of hope (which has nothing to do with despair); a continual rejection (which cannot be confused with renunciation); and a conscious dissatisfaction (which must not be compared to immature unrest)." "Everything considered, a determined soul will

always manage." For, to "say that life is absurd, the conscience must be alive." And a living conscience leads a man
to confront, without blinders of any kind—metaphysical,
religious, or ideological—an absurd political situation.

The very qualities so many think they see in Camus's
work, and find so attractive about it, a stylish despair and
a mature unrest, the man himself specifically disowns.
"The idea that a pessimistic philosophy is necessarily one
of discouragement," he wrote in *Combat* in September
1945, "is a puerile idea." Nor was Camus an orthodox Existentialist. In the same piece he wrote that he did "not
have much liking for the too famous existential philosophy,
and, to tell the truth, I think its conclusions false. But at
least it represents a great adventure of the mind." Nor
again was Camus's acceptance of the Absurd a matter of
formal philosophic commitment. "No, everything is not
summed up in negation and absurdity. We know this. But
we must first posit negation and absurdity because they are
what our generation has encountered and we must take
into account." What *is* at the bottom of his commitment is
that, everything considered, a determined soul will always
manage. The whole thrust of his work, and his life, is towards existing *within* messiness, learning to live in the *absence* of assurance that one is right and one's opponent
wrong.

"I know," he says, "that in order to keep alive, the absurd must not be settled." In order for freedom to be kept
alive—for the political solution to be left open, devoid of
absolute demands, and daily recreated—politics must not,
in this sense, be settled once and for all. That does not
mean that the Algerian problem defies settlement, but that

settlement has to be earned rather than imposed by fiat. Every claim must be listened to, every aspiration taken into account, every nuance weighed. It is in character for Camus to choose as a frontispiece for the volume which contains some of his most haunting papers on Algeria a quotation from Pascal: "A man does not show his greatness by being at one extremity, but rather by touching both at once." Camus does his utmost to touch both extremities at once in the Algerian situation, both French and Arab feelings, demands, recriminations, and ideals, and to seek limits within the situation itself. "To begin with," he writes, "I lack the assurance that allows one to settle everything" —especially when what he writes "in the comfort of the study," stemming from abstract principles and risking nothing, "might provide an alibi for the insane criminal who may throw his bomb into an innocent crowd that includes my family."

Now all this sounds rather dramatic. But if a person is unable to locate a corresponding stirring within himself he is not likely to appreciate Camus's political science, or even to understand it. Every time Camus writes, he is in danger of providing the alibi for an insane criminal to throw his bomb into an innocent crowd that includes his family. For Camus to write at all, then, is a terrible responsibility. But anytime anybody writes—and that is part of the lesson Camus hopes to impress upon us—he is in danger of providing the alibi for a criminal such as Stalin or Hitler or Mao, or those who managed French imperialism in Algeria or the American "presence" in Vietnam. And that also is a terrible responsibility. The lesson, however, is not yet complete. Any time any of us votes, not in the comfort of the study, but in the anonymity of the voting booth, we run the risk as well of providing the alibi for just such an insane criminal to hurl his bomb—or his hate or dogma —into an innocent crowd which includes the families of others. And that, too, is a terrible responsibility.

Yet Camus's political dilemma is hardly a simple either-or question. One who has gone beyond the first stages of rebellion, who has passed through the earliest phase of dawning awareness, does not put the question in terms of all-or-nothing. If anyone "thinks heroically that one's brother must die, rather than one's principles, I shall go no farther than to admire him from a distance. I am not of his stamp." Some actually believe that it is more difficult to be a saint than to be a human being. Camus, like Orwell, is of the opinion that striving for sainthood can be far simpler than accepting the burdens of one's own humanity.* On the other hand, that "does not mean that principles have no meaning." The point is that both loyalties exist, both exert their several claims, both must be kept alive: one's brother and one's principles. The belief is that by agreeing on limits—not on giving up the struggle for freedom and justice—but on limits such as, to cite only the most primitive case, rules of warfare, there is still a chance to keep one's brother and one's principles alive. The true horror is to be forced to choose either one's brother or one's principles. In that event, it seems clear Camus would choose his brother.

In his philosophical essays Camus expresses the self-

---

*"I don't want to be a philosophical genius. I don't want to be a genius at all, I have enough trouble just being a man." *Notebooks, 1942–1951* (1966), p. 135.

same doubt of his own omniscience, and his suspicion of principles not firmly bound to this earth and tempered by earthly considerations. He would, if he must choose, always prefer life to inexorable principle. But again, he would wish to make no exclusive choice but to maintain a blend of creature and creation, feeling and reason, character and community. In *The Rebel* he says, "To abandon oneself to principles is really to die—and to die for an impossible love, which is the contrary of love." Abandon oneself to principles? One must recognize that a human being is superior to any principle. "Does the end justify the means?" he asks. May principles ever justify the actual deeds of men? Camus answers, "That is possible. But what will justify the end? To that question [I reply]: the means." And in *The Myth of Sisyphus* he writes, "That universal reason, practical or ethical, that determinism, those categories that explain everything, are enough to make a decent man laugh,"—provided they didn't lead to so many tragic misunderstandings, to so much wasteful strife, in the end to brutality and murder, which are enough to make anybody weep.

But the real question in Algeria, however much the inflexibles on either side argued that it was a matter of principle or of honor, was "not how to die separately, but rather how to live together." He writes to an Arab, like himself a seeker after some basis for solution, "We are condemned to live together." This is as succinct a statement of Camus's theory of community as I have found in his writings. *We are condemned to live together*: the theme of practically every novel and short story he composed. But why "condemned," why not "blessed" to live together? To respond to this objection is to restate the human condition from the perspective of the community: because you and I are different. We are different persons, with different skins, legatees of different histories, worshipping different gods, speaking different tongues, entertaining different aspirations. These differences tempt some of us to feel superior to the rest, to believe, in Camus's words, that we are beneficiaries of "some kind of revelation of the truth." Yet the only truth is that the personal history of each of us is "but the story, if it could be truthfully written, . . . of successive lapses, sometimes corrected, and committed once again." Once we relinquish the preposterous claim to know the "truth," however, we immediately place ourselves, vis-à-vis those who are positive they do know it, in an absurd position. For they will scorn us as fools. Yet, what else is there to do?

Camus's position, as it relates specifically to the Algerian situation, is set forth in these words: what it amounts to is "taking one's stand in the no man's land, between two armies, and preaching amid the bullets that war is a deception. . . . If anyone dares to put his whole heart and all his suffering into such a cry, he will hear in reply nothing but laughter, and a louder clash of arms. And yet we must cry it aloud, . . . [we must do this] mad and necessary thing." The laughter he would provoke recalls the scornful laughter which dogged the steps of the holy fool of earlier times and served to hearten him.

Put all one's heart and suffering into a cry for moderation? All one's passion in a plea against unreasonable and dangerous passions? Even though men will not listen, and if they do listen, will not heed? Stand in no man's land, pleading for limits amid the whizzing bullets? Camus feels he must do this "mad and necessary thing." In the relationship between the mad and the necessary lies Camus's theory of rebellion, ultimately his hopes for fashioning a set of political limits applicable to the conduct of modern men.

The maxim of Pascal which Camus admired and which he attempted to honor in his conduct reads: "A man does not show his greatness by being at one extremity, but rather by touching both at once." To resort to an analogy, a complete and utter break with the past, say in painting, is not actually too difficult to achieve. We simply ignore all limits to form set in nature and in the history of painting and subject the world to our own invention. But it is no easier than stylized representational painting, which does not begin to do justice to the power of human inventiveness. The trick is to respect nature, then edit her; to accept tradition, then point the way to a more imaginative future.

Camus's intention is to touch both extremities at once, in hopes of achieving a creative continuity. He aims at that change which would nourish the best of both, and withholds approval from all change that would submerge one in the other. What he struggles above all to attain, whether or not his grasp is as sure as his reach, is no desolate compromise, but an expression in word and deed of the complementarity of life: love *and* justice, men *and* principles, the French *and* the Arabs—Algeria.

Ideally this would not resemble the reflexive conduct of the born or machine-tooled moderate, but would be the choice of a free man, one who is capable of touching both extremities at the same time; a man who tries to bear within his being the principles, perspectives, tastes, smells, the sights and sounds of us all. He takes his stand in the no man's land between the armies and preaches amid the bullets that war itself is a deception. And he fully expects his cries to set the adversaries to peals of derisive laughter. For he himself is also the adversary, and how often Albert must have laughed at Camus.

In *The Myth of Sisyphus* he writes, "The absurd is lucid reason noting its own limits." The absurd "establishes its limits, since it is powerless to calm its anguish." The absurd establishes its limits because its unfortunate adherents view the universe as neither rational nor irrational. They live in anguish with a fateful question to which there can be no definitive answer. Camus quotes with approval the famous line of Pindar: "O my soul, do not aspire to immortal life, but exhaust the limits of the possible." We begin to draw within earshot of that cry of anguish from no man's land. It is the "Nothing too much" of the ancient Greeks, glimpsed through the prism of Montaigne's "Je m'abstein" and presented as a gift to contemporary humanity. It is, explore the limits of the possible, explore life, seek the boundaries of existence, but be prepared to pay up for your own extravagances. From the standpoint of modern political thought, this ancient idea of limits is, ironically, Camus's most interesting idea.

Against those who contend that life is meaningless and that suicide is as rational a response as any other, namely, the modern nihilists; against those who contend that life is meaningless unless history contains value, and who believe that in certain situations murder may be condoned, namely, the modern revolutionaries; against those who contend that life, on the contrary, is objectively meaningful and must be lived in a certain way, namely, the true believers of whatever religious faith—against all, Camus argues that the life of man is neither meaningless nor beyond accident: instead, the basic ineluctable fact is that man finds himself in a "limited situation." This limited situation is imposed upon us by the nature of things. Camus derives his idea of limits not from ethical or historical inquiry exclusively, nor from philosophy proper, but from the very physical and psychological limitations of human existence: the physical fact that we are mortal, the psychological fact that we live and create life in spite of it.

The true rebel begins his rebellion by insisting upon the "facts" of human limitation. He says in effect, You are not a god but a mortal like myself. I am, therefore, inviolable as you, and you are inviolable as I. Thus far shall you go, but no farther. There is a limit beyond which you cannot go without forfeiting both my humanity and your own, my integrity and yours, my freedom and your freedom. A borderline exists in human relations corresponding to the borderline in man's relation to the physical universe, including his human condition. Cross that borderline, transcend those limits, and you kill me or you will be killed. In either event you destroy yourself.

The problem is that from Camus's standpoint one must rebel before one begins to exist as an identity, as a free agent in the world. But the rebel is apt to lose sight of the fact that others exist in the world also. Too seldom does he respect the existence of those others by limiting his own rebellious actions. It is for all of us a great joy to witness a justified, particularly a long overdue, rebellion such as that of the tentative young person against parental authority, and the exhilaration that accompanies that first No. "From now on I'll make my own decisions for myself, I'll live my own life and accept responsibility for my own conduct." Marvelous. But Camus would remind us that life is no light comedy, over in two hours' time. The danger inherent in rebellion is that it might be self-perpetuating and become a style of response, a thing-in-itself, finally a mere reflex. Too often "rebellion, forgetful of its generous origins, allows itself to be contaminated by resentment; it denies life, dashes towards destruction. . . . It is no longer . . . rebellion but rancor, malice, and tyranny." For what of the suffering of the other, what of *his* identity, *his* humanity? The parent is not merely a despot, but a maternal or paternal lover as well which, I suppose, partly accounts for the belated nature of most such rebellions. Perhaps the Absurd is best expressed in that—almost inevitable—human circumstance in which the parent is also a child, the child also a parent. The only principle one may appropriately derive from a condition in which one is at the same time both Authority and potential Rebel is compassion. To Camus rebellion is no synonym for vengeance, it is a coming of age. He argues not that the Arabs must now get back their own in some fantastical way, but that they must assert their mature freedom, which is another way for Camus to speak of limits.

Rebellion, however it presents itself to the actual or potential rebel, is still a social phenomenon and always involves the other. Even our deepest silence is a social stance. Whether we wish it or not, whether, indeed, we like it or not, all our actions affect other flesh-and-blood beings. Whenever we neglect to consider this, we exceed the limits of our humanness and adopt a hostile stance toward our fellows, pridefully inconsiderate of the race of men. We become as gods, in opposition to "the only original rule of life today: to learn to live and to die, and, in order to be a man, to refuse to be a god." Always whether "By our silence, or by the stand we take, we . . . enter the fray."

Camus is not trying to put over that most banal of arguments, that we are all guilty, all murderers, and none is more responsible than the rest. In that event it could truly be said that all is permitted, for none may be isolated from the whole and brought to judgment. What he does say is that if "rebellion could found a philosophy, it would be a philosophy of limits, of calculated ignorance, or risk. He who does not know everything, cannot kill everything." The theoretician who saw in the nations of Southeast Asia a row of dominoes ready to collapse serially at the first push knew everything, and killed everything he could. The revolutionary who sees in American society today merely a replica of the fascist state of the thirties knows everything, and plants his bombs. Such persons imagine that only they are in touch with reality; the rest of us they regard as either fools or knaves. But *he who does not know everything, cannot kill everything.*

Camus opts for a philosophy of limits, of calculated ignorance, and of risk. The ignorance we can see, the limits we can see; but where does the risk lie? Precisely in the fact that by our silence we also enter the fray. Thus by preaching ultimate ignorance and inherent limits, Camus has no intention of letting us off the hook. His is not the counsel of complacency. On the contrary, since whether we care to or not we enter the fray, it would pay us well to attempt to understand our own attachments and prejudices, and the likely consequences of our actions. The worth of a man is "measured by the extent" to which he has rejected complacency by refusing to retreat into "a position of arbitrary barrenness." Unthinking moderation is mediocrity; unthinking extremism is mediocrity; unthinking withdrawal is mediocrity. They are but different forms of arbitrary barrenness. Respect for human limits, regardless of the specific strategy involved—whether withdrawal or direct action or mediation—constitutes a rejection of complacency. So there we have it: passion and reason; rebellion and limits; the Rebel's determination to enter the fray, if only to become human, and his compelling sense of his own ignorance, partiality, and ambiguity.

There may be detected in everything Camus has written a certain pride. Perhaps he would defend it as the justifiable pride of mortal men pitted against the destructive pride of those who would be as gods. Such mortal pride is necessary to sustain us in what Camus hopes will be our stubborn resistance as we face "the tremendous tension created by refusing to give a positive or negative answer," our resistance against finally abandoning ourselves "to complete negation or total submission." There is, he states quietly, "no possible salvation for the man who feels real compassion." Savor the pride of those words! We have here not the response of Ivan Karamazov—"I rejoice that there will be no salvation for me, for I would sooner live as a super-human Devil, than exist as a dependent mortal like the rest of the cattle; I crave greatness, that is my true secret"—but the pride of the man who already sees the greatness of being simply, but fully, a man. If there is no salvation for such a one as Camus, he also believes that there is no salvation for any of us, whether by submitting to a political dogma or prostrating ourselves before a leader.

"One leader, one people," he says in *The Rebel*, "signifies one master and millions of slaves. The political mediaries . . . are in all societies, the guarantors of freedom." Not uniformity, but diversity is what requires protection, even loving care: diversity in race, diversity in traditions, diversity in talents, diversity in goals, diversity in temperament and in character. Camus not only accepts diversity as, say, an empirical political scientist accepts the "reality" of pluralism in American society and politics, he is its champion. Nor does he accept diversity only out of fear that unless we do accept it, political strife will tear us apart. Rather Camus is arguing that with the disappearance or suppression of differences, the world becomes immeasurably poorer. Meanwhile the mediaries—political actors, groups and societies, fraternities and associations and institutions—are not simply there, but there as guarantors of our freedom. Camus's political slogan, applied to large communities, might properly read: Unity always, totality never. Referring to Algeria, with its French and Arabs, but also its Turks, its Berbers, and its Jews, Camus said, "here, as in every domain, I believe only in differences, and not in uniformity."

Camus entertained a profound respect for the complementarity of existence. In the realm of the political, complementarity would appear to demand the diversity of the many within the community of the many, a most difficult, even heartbreaking ideal, particularly where the differences are profound. "In a world entirely dominated by history, which ours threatens to become, there are no longer any mistakes, but only crimes, of which the greatest is moderation." What is more, no sooner do you express such an ideal than it sounds second-rate really, so mediocre: intermediary groups, associations and fraternities, not to mention mayors and city councils and committees, patient political education and patient political negotiation. No wonder one's opponents are tempted to laugh one to scorn. For they have all the answers. Unfortunately, they also have the guns. ("Virtue is not learned so rapidly as the handling of a submachine gun. The fight is unequal.") Camus stands not in the political center, but in the no man's land and cries aloud that political absolutes are a deception.*

In each of the attitudes and responses to the complexities of politics, I find Camus's Rebel to be the ideal of Political Man in the modern world. In the absence of fixed principles, he nevertheless cherishes unity and distrusts uniformity, respects diversity but resists violent and mutually destructive conflict, appreciates ambiguity and resists the tempting counsel either of renunciation or of contempt. Camus's Political Man respects men and distrusts mankind, as well as the determined lovers of mankind who commit the most heinous crimes in our name. He confesses

---

*In the game he loved so to play, soccer, Camus's position was goalie, which should come as no great surprise. He frequently remarked that he had learned far more philosophy on the playing field than he ever had in the classroom. His later aspirations as a writer only served to strengthen his conviction that the place for him to take his stand was in no man's land. "The writer condemned to *understanding*," he wrote in his notebook, "He cannot be a killer." *Notebooks, 1942 –1951*, p. 195.

ignorance, and suspects the neat solution. He combines an attachment to flesh-and-blood human beings with an attachment to principles, and frankly acknowledges the difficulty of choosing between them in any given situation. Thus the Political Man looks to circumstances rather than to abstractions. He yearns to explore the limits of the possible in political affairs and is wary of his own tendency to fall into bad faith. Finally, he does not live as anyone's slave.

What it all adds up to is a defiance of political fatalism by Camus, and a consequent openness to possibility. Determinism in human affairs, whatever the source and whatever the aims, is a flight from responsibility in a world bereft of certitude. Man is not a "piece of fatality," unless he chooses to believe as much. In an appeal from a public platform in Algeria in 1956—surely a political no man's land—Camus said:

> People are too readily resigned to fatality. They are too ready to believe that, after all, nothing but bloodshed makes history progress and that the stronger always progresses at the expense of the weaker. Such fatality exists perhaps. But man's task is not to accept it or bow to its laws. If he had accepted it in the earliest ages, we should still be living in prehistoric times. The task of men of culture and faith, in any case, is not to desert historical struggles nor to serve the cruel and inhuman elements in those struggles. It is rather to remain what they are, to help man against what is oppressing

him, to favor freedom against the fatalities that close in upon it.

That is the condition under which history really progresses, innovates—in a word, creates. In everything else it repeats itself, like a bleeding mouth that merely vomits forth a wild stammering.

The modern State created in the imagination of Machiavelli and equipped with sovereignty and citizenship by Hobbes and Rousseau has, in our time, become a horror. But the more we have attempted to strip its claims bare, the more we have undermined its rationale, the more power it seems to have accrued and the more impersonally brutal it has become. Paradoxically, the Nazi and Fascist and Communist states are inconceivable without the mining and sapping work of the thinkers of the nineteenth century, who thought to purchase our freedom from the tyrant. Machiavelli, Hobbes, and Rousseau had been writing out of a different context, political chaos or corruption, in the hopes of creating an instrument capable of controlling meaningless violence and selfishness. In this way they were reacting "dialectically" with reality, as were the great unmaskers of the nineteenth century. The West today suffers from a want of meaning and, at the same time, from a profound fear, for good reason, of the holistic system and the mystique of authority.

No Prince, no Sovereign, no General Will structures our existence and imparts meaning to political life. The man and the woman find themselves once again naked in the Garden, at evening time, and hide themselves in their shame as they await the Voice. That is why I find Camus's courageous effort to establish limits, however difficult in practice, even utopian, so moving. We no longer have the luxury of thinking to deploy violence and deceit in order to establish unity, as did Machiavelli. We are conscious enough not to join in an attempt at blackmail in order to still the conscience of men, as with Hobbes. We are too aware of the political history of our own time to believe in the possibility of creating an organic community, such as that of Rousseau. Either the effort will fail or, should it succeed, will perhaps infect the modern world with still another example of a monstrously distorted *gemeinschaft*. In our nakedness, and our shame, the only possibility for the political theorist is to give himself wholeheartedly to the project of inventing a set of limits to political action. I say inventing, for the mystiques of solace resorted to by those political theorists who were responsible for the creation and maintenance of the tradition are no longer available to us. Besides, there is no possible salvation for the soul that truly feels compassion.

Epilogue

THE course of this book has transcribed a noble arc, from the lowest metaphysical and political pandering of earlier times to the highest theoretical chastity in our own day. The reader, presumably like the author, is confirmed thereby and rushes to declare himself among the company of the unsolaced, the only honorable place for the disenchanted but undaunted spirit to take up a stand. Yet nothing—except perhaps the obverse, playing the role of Grand Inquisitor to the lower orders of humanity—could be more prideful.

George Orwell's insistence that human beings are not failed saints but creatures used and broken up by life, which is nothing less than their loving attachment to other flesh and blood people like themselves; Hannah Arendt's modest desire simply to prevent catastrophes where possible, or maybe only to mitigate their effects; and Albert Camus's assertion that he wished merely to be a man above all, and not a special genius, are no doubt sincere. Their Stoicism is real, their courage extraordinary, their separation from the rest of us by virtue of that very attitude, profound. Even when viewed not as arrogant but admirable, their stance is nonetheless elitist, removed from the capacities of many of us to emulate.

And that is a shame. For their message is of the utmost

urgency, especially today; beware the easy deal, measure well the costs of any political theory offering solace which, if understood in full, may prove unconscionable. Yet these three thinkers, obviously my personal culture heroes and the source of much inspiration for my own ideas, went beyond that salutary caution. They appear to judge the very need for solace a glaring weakness of character. Whatever his intentions, each in his thought removed himself by that much from the thick of the perennial human struggle, the necessity both for shaping a unique identity and for sharing ourselves with others. The paradox is that, again whatever his intentions, each was in the solace business himself, and in the finest possible way, actually demanding very little of our freedom of conscience in return.

There is, Camus had written, no possible salvation for the truly compassionate soul, bad news indeed for humanity; no salvation by imputing a positive meaning to the universe, or positive values natural to human life. Conversely, even the most deeply struck pessimism is unwarranted, for it must necessarily impute the meaning at least of non-meaning to the world. What exists instead is but cosmic indifference, directionless drift, profound individual solitude. In the face of this horror we are enjoined, all of us, to create out of the chaos, out of the void even, and to bless the good fortune which has seen the rubbish of the past swept away before our eyes for the first time in over two thousand years. Such would appear to be the message of Orwell, Arendt and Camus. All of it, all those centuries of thought, systems, dreams and splendid visions, all have come down quite simply to this: universal shipwreck followed by darkness as pitch black as the ages ever knew—

*certainly a challenge worthy of the modern political theo-
rist with no tricks up his sleeve.*

*Yet, as I have tried to suggest, to read anything com-
posed by Orwell or Arendt or Camus is to be solaced. What
else is writing for others, the sharing if need be of one's
own specially terrifying nightmares, than the offering up
of solace to one's fellows? It is form that supplies the structure which imparts meaning to existence. Even to read
"there exists no meaning, we are all lost," is to have something. To be human, one requires not the hope of salvation
but the continuing experience of solace. Moreover, to remain human, to stay alive at all, one must also have pride.
By pride I do not mean hubris, the overweening pride
which tempts a man to think himself God, but the mortal
pride that refuses to be broken upon the rocks of adversity.*

*Reverse the order of Camus's observation that there
exists no salvation for the truly compassionate soul, and
much of what is at stake in political theory and action becomes accessible: he who holds out the promise to others
of salvation in this world cannot possibly be possessed of
a compassionate soul. The cost of the object of such a "love"
comes always too dear, calling forth a sacrifice in the can-
didate for salvation, namely, his right in the future to judge
for himself. Consign your judgment to the Leader or the
Movement, to the Idea or the System, once and for all, and
be saved. Kafka once wrote that we may choose not to suffer, but that such a choice might well turn out to be the
last one we'll ever make.*

*To be human means to stand in need of solace, of com-
fort in our grief or loss or in the painful throes of anxiety.
What is unacceptable in the settlement drawn up in our*

behalf, say, by Thomas Hobbes, is not that the promise of
solace was held out, but that the cost for attaining it was
debilitating. In acquiescing, we make a gift to the Sovereign—or the political theorist—of our profoundest political
judgment. We become less than human. Solace, then, demands a price. But it need not be one as high as that insisted upon by Hobbes—which was, in a word, renunciation. On the contrary, the price demanded by solace may
vary both with circumstances and with the character of the
parties to the exchange. That is, we need not abandon altogether our desire for solace just because the history of the
consequences of that desire has so often proved it deadly,
fueling as it has the cruel ambitions of tyrants along with
their retinues of trained seals, the scribes.

The antidote to surrendering up one's judgment to the
safekeeping of others has everywhere and always been the
determination to think for oneself. The cost to the serious
reader of the solace dispensed by Orwell, Arendt, and Camus is thinking—precisely the activity from which presumably it is necessary to have respite, and on whose account,
above all other activities, we require solace in the first
place. So many stand ready to relieve us of our brains. "Oh,
how soft and pleasant and healthful a pillow, whereon to
rest a prudent head, is ignorance and lack of curiosity!"
exclaimed Montaigne. To rouse ourselves up from our slum-
ber by taking thought is painful, perhaps even "unnatural."
But deliberately to experience the pain in concert with our
fellows, and to share our perceptions of meaning, however
fleeting or partial, amidst confusion and despair is to be
solaced, and at a price which, unbearable as it might seem,
saves us from resigning our powers of decision to others.

Orwell, Arendt, and Camus were right in refusing to join uncritically a tradition in which solace was a good to be purchased at almost any price. They were not right when, on occasion, they exhibited that more-than-human pride in their own capacity to face horrors sufficient to send the common run of humanity fleeing in panic. Stoicism in the modern world, as most of Existentialism, potentially breeds an elitist arrogance by the elegant rejection of any solace whatever. It grows fat upon aesthetic nourishment alone. But to read and write and think, like Orwell, Arendt, and Camus at their best, is to receive and to offer solace at the only cost which does not impair our compassion for other flesh-and-blood human beings like ourselves: it is to see through their eyes and to feel with their hearts.

A final feature of the thought of Arendt and Camus particularly, and of the practice of Orwell, is its comple-mentarity, the insistence upon not ruling a serious idea or program out of contention, in principle, but attempting to adapt its best characteristics, in the process placing other ideas and programs in a novel perspective each to the others. To all three of them, exclusion was inevitably im-poverishment, for no single theory or plan of action is suf-ficient unto itself to comprehend the varieties of human experience and invention. "A mind somewhat accustomed to the gymnastics of intelligence knows, like Pascal, that all error comes from an exclusion," Camus wrote in the Note-books. *"Nietzsche's experience added to ours, like Pascal's added to Darwin's, Callicles's added to Plato's, restores the whole human register and returns us to our native land." The whole human voice, nothing left out, is what it will take to remove us from the wilderness of political indiffer-*

ence or of political murder, and lead us back home. Then, with characteristic caution following so sweeping an assertion, there follows the inevitable qualifier: "But all this can be true only with a dozen additional reservations" (p. 59). In an age of scientific conceit and ideological certitude, how reassuring is the appearance of any qualification whatever, particularly in the text of a political writer. And how solacing to those temperaments which greet each novel claim and spectacular promise with a dread shiver of recognition.